THE MEANING OF GOD

The Meaning of God

Robert H. King

FORTRESS PRESS
PHILADELPHIA

Library of Congress Catalog Card Number 73-80635

ISBN 0-8006-0257-9

3852D73 Printed in U.S.A. 1-257

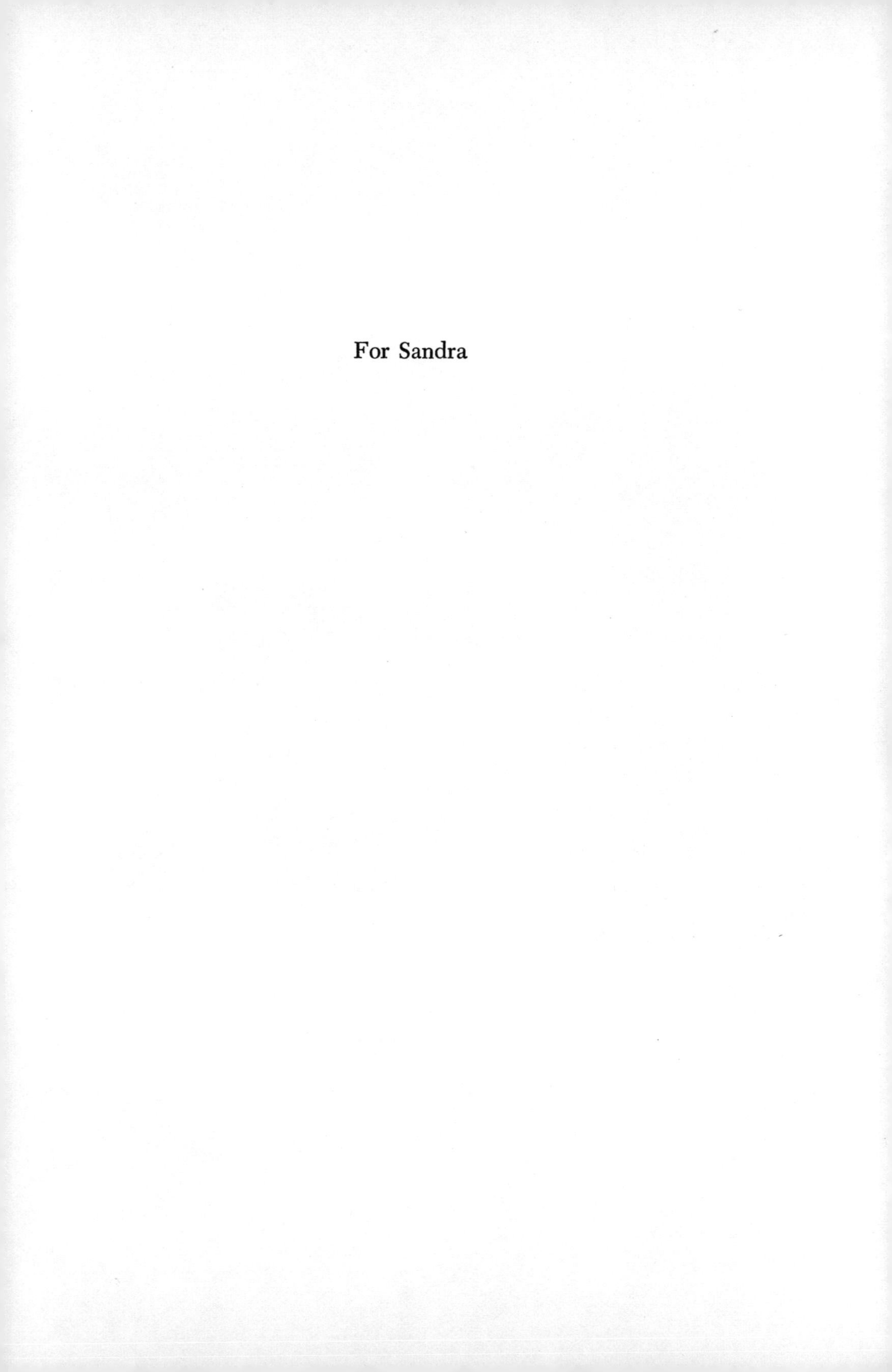

For Sandra

CONTENTS

PREFACE

In the continuing dialogue between Western philosophy and the Christian religion, the central issue has frequently been the existence of God. Yet in recent years the focus of the discussion has shifted to the meaning of "God." This is a quite different question, and a more basic one. For if it is meaningless to speak of God, the question of his existence or nonexistence does not even arise. It is possible simply to dismiss this whole way of speaking.

Even within the church there is confusion and uncertainty about what it means to speak of God. Our tradition has bequeathed to us a certain way of speaking; yet confronted with many alternatives (including that of not speaking of God at all), we wonder sometimes if we really know what it all means. When we say that God creates and sustains the world, that he actively intervenes in the affairs of men, and that he has a purpose which far surpasses anything we can conceive of, do we know what we are talking about? Can we fit this in with our other ways of thinking and speaking, or is it simply a residue of some earlier time no longer meaningful in our time?

These are important questions arising out of a situation of religious pluralism and secularization yet having significance in their own right. For if there is any one concept that is basic to the Christian tradition, it is the concept of God. In getting clear about the meaning of "God," we establish a basis for dealing with other questions which might arise within this tradition. We lay the groundwork for a systematic theology. It would seem imperative, therefore, that theology come to terms with this issue, that it provide some answer to the question of what it *means* to speak of God.

As a way of coming at this question, I have drawn heavily upon the work of analytical philosophers such as Wittgenstein, Ryle, Strawson, and Anscombe—not for what they say about God but for the insight they provide into the concepts by which we speak of God. All talk about God is, after all, analogical, so we might as well consider the material from which the primary analogies are drawn. In that way we may hope to gain some perspective on our subject. My contention is that a concept of God consistent with biblical tradition and congruent with our other ways of speaking is possible. It may diverge in certain respects from the traditional view, yet it need not be totally at variance with it to be meaningful within the present context.

The development of the argument set forth in this book took place over many years so that the list of those who have assisted in one way or another would be far too long to cite. I would, however, like to mention two individuals who have been particularly influential in the development of my thought. One is Austin Farrer, to whose theological writings I continually return for instruction and inspiration. The other is Hans Frei, whose constant encouragement and friendly criticism have sustained me through many a dry spell and steered me past some major pitfalls. In the latter stages of the project, I also received useful suggestions and criticisms from two of my DePauw colleagues, John Eigenbrodt and Roger Gustavsson, and from Ian Barbour and Robert Off.

I am indebted to the National Endowment for the Humanities, the Great Lakes Colleges Association–Carnegie Humanities Program, and DePauw University for grants which made it possible for me to spend a profitable year of study in Oxford, England, during 1967–68. An abbreviated version of the argument in this book appears in my article, "The Conceivability of God" (*Religious Studies*, March 1973).

The book is dedicated to my wife, Sandra, who has been a faithful companion in dialogue and discovery throughout the time that I have been at work on this project. It would be difficult to conceive of apart from our shared experiences during those years.

Robert H. King

1. THE SECULAR CHALLENGE TO RELIGION

Religion is a basic human enterprise. Every culture we encounter seems to exhibit some characteristics of religion. These characteristics are diverse. They include such matters as corporate worship, private meditation, cosmological speculation, and moral exhortation. Yet for all their diversity, they seem to present an identifiable pattern: we are able to speak of some things as religions. No one seriously disputes, for instance, that Hinduism, Buddhism, and Christianity are religions. To say what it is they all have in common is another matter, however, and a subject of some dispute.

In the modern era, we have become particularly self-conscious concerning religion. Confrontation with other cultures has made us aware of fundamental religious differences. No longer is it possible to appeal uncritically to one's own religious tradition as though it constituted the sole religious perspective. We have been forced to acknowledge that there are many ways of being religious—some of them very different from our own. But that is not all. We have also had to reckon with the possibility of dispensing with religion altogether. Increasingly, it seems, we are confronted by persons who express no need for religion, who even consider it a hindrance to their quest for a full and meaningful life. For them the choice is not between competing sects within a single religion, or even between two totally different religions, but between religion of any sort and a thoroughgoing secularism.

This is the context within which we have to consider the question of God. It is a context at once pluralistic and secular. It is pluralistic in that it includes radically different religious systems competing for the allegiances of men, secular in that it admits of the possibility of dispensing with religious systems altogether. Such a context poses a particular challenge to religion, since it calls in question the most basic assumptions of a religion. But it also provides an occasion for examining these assumptions. It forces us to think about what we *mean* when we speak in this way. That could in the long run be a benefit to religion.

THE PROBLEM OF TRANSCENDENCE

A satisfactory definition of religion is not readily at hand. It is even questionable whether one can be given in view of the great diversity exhibited by actual religions. Yet some attempt must be made in that direction if we are to talk at all meaningfully about the secular challenge to religion. Let us begin then by saying that whatever else religion is it is a "form of life." It is a way of "being in the world." The term *form of life* comes from the philosopher Wittgenstein, who recognized that all language has its setting in the activities of people. If we want to understand what certain words mean, we must observe how they are used in the actual conduct of life.[1] Religious ways of speaking are no exception: they too have their meaning in relationship to a form of life.

If anything, the relationship is more explicit than with certain other ways of speaking. That is because it is one of the functions of religious language to articulate a way of life, to make explicit assumptions, beliefs, and attitudes which might otherwise remain implicit. One way in which this is done is by projecting an "ideal of life." The ideal may be individual or social; it may be expressed in legend, myth, or ritual; it may permeate an entire culture or be confined to a single sect; it will in any case make a profound difference for the people involved. It will affect the way in which they conceive of themselves and their world, and thus influence the way they live their lives. For man does not live by bread alone. He is dependent upon meanings of an inclusive sort (ideals, aspirations, hopes, and the like) to give direction and significance to what he does. Religion is a principal source and depository of these meanings.

There is, of course, no one religious ideal. The ideals which have at one time or another been associated with religion vary all the way from ascetic self-denial to robust celebration of the earthy qualities of life. They include the ideal of a society based upon absolute equality and that of strict hierarchical order. Sometimes the ideal of service to others has been dominant; other times it has been communion with nature, meditation upon the self, or some other activity that has been the focus of attention. Yet whatever the ideal, it has made a difference in people's lives—not only in the sense that it has given them a goal to work toward, but also in the sense that it has given them something to

1. Ludwig Wittgenstein, *Philosophical Investigations* (New York: Macmillan, 1953), pars. 19, 23, p. 226.

hope for. Religion is as much concerned with men's expectations as with their aspirations.

But then this can be said of many things other than simply religion.[2] In literature and the arts, in politics and economics, even in the realm of science, various ideals of life are set forth and adhered to—sometimes in ways very much like what one finds in religion. There are, for instance, rituals, myths, and creeds which express the ideals of a nation, class, or culture, just as there are for religion. In addition, there are rules to be followed, conventions to be adhered to, and symbols to be respected. If the most that we can say about religion is that it articulates a form of life, then we shall not have succeeded to any significant extent in distinguishing religious expression from other forms of expression. There must be something that is distinctive about religion. I would argue that it is the element of transcendence.

Whenever a person speaks religiously, he speaks not only of what is observable but of what is beyond observation, not only of what is a part of the world but of what transcends it. This can be seen in religions as diverse as Buddhism and Christianity. Buddha, for instance, did not believe in God, or at least did not encourage such a belief among his followers, yet the concept of Nirvana which he espoused is fully as elusive, mysterious, and transcendent as anything to be found in Christianity. To the extent that it can be spoken of at all, it can only be spoken of dialectically or in parables. (One is reminded of the way in which Jesus spoke of the Kingdom of God—almost always in parables, metaphors, and images, never by way of direct description.)

Yet it might be argued that what is really distinctive about the teachings of both Buddha and Christ is the emphasis placed upon salvation, the need for and promise of deliverance from an undesirable situation into a desirable one. Buddha speaks of the universality of suffering and holds out the prospect for an end to suffering. Christ calls for repentance in anticipation of the coming of God's reign. Both insist that all other interests should be subordinate to this one overriding concern—whether it be thought of as enlightenment or redemption. The concept of salvation, however, involves transcendence. It would not be the concept it is without this element. It would simply be another scheme for self-improvement or for the amelioration of social

2. Compare P. F. Strawson, "Social Morality and the Individual Ideal," *Christian Ethics and Contemporary Philosophy*, ed. Ian Ramsey (New York: Macmillan, 1966).

ills. The kind of deliverance Buddhists and Christians alike are concerned with is a deliverance which goes beyond what is observable, verifiable, or even fully realizable under present conditions. It is an elusive, far-reaching hope, one which can only be called transcendent.

The concept of God, though not always present in religion, epitomizes this dimension of transcendence. It brings to focal awareness what would otherwise be only implicit in concepts such as enlightenment, redemption, and salvation. It is for that reason the religious concept *par excellence*. But it is also more problematical than other concepts, more difficult to relate to other ways of speaking, and less obvious in its reference. When we speak of God, we make explicit what is most elusive and mysterious in religion. We enter into the area of greatest controversy—particularly in a "secular age" such as ours. For if there is one thing that is antithetical to the secular mind it is the notion of transcendence epitomized by the concept of God.

Were we to look upon religion simply as a form of life, or possibly as a form of life with salvation as its objective, the concept of God would not figure so prominently in our thinking. But then neither would we be so disposed to look upon this as a secular age. The church as an institution may not be so influential as it once was. Certain conventional forms of religious expression may be less in evidence than at some earlier time. But there is no lack of "systems of salvation"—ranging all of the way from psychotherapy to communal living. The absence of the transcendent makes this a secular age (if indeed it is). Our general inability to find meaning at this particular level disposes us to think of ourselves as less than religious—and that it is as true for persons within the church as for those outside. The loss of a sense of the transcendent affects us all.

There are no doubt ways of regarding the phenomenon of secularity other than simply as a loss of transcendent meaning,[3] but this is how I would like to think of it. The "secular challenge," as I see it, is a challenge to the meaningfulness of religious discourse, particularly as it relates to the transcendent. Since transcendence is basic to any sort of religious meaning, the secular challenge strikes at the foundations of the religious enterprise. It would be difficult to conceive of a more serious threat. At the same time, however, it provides an occasion for looking more closely at the meaning of this way of thinking, speaking,

3. See especially Peter Berger, *The Sacred Canopy* (New York: Doubleday, 1969) and Thomas Luckmann, *The Invisible Religion* (New York: Macmillan, 1967).

and behaving. The secular point of view, just because it calls into question what is most basic to religion, could provide a useful perspective upon religion. It could lead to greater religious self-understanding. But before we proceed further in that direction, we need to consider what it is about the transcendent which makes it seem meaningless to so many people at this time.

One way of approaching this question would be along the lines of the Marxist critique of religion. Marx considered religion meaningless because it alienated a person from himself. Human good transcendently conceived was, in his judgment, human good cut off from its source in the social life of man and made inaccessible to the very persons for whom it was meant. A classic example of this alienation is the Christian promise of heavenly gratification to those who suffer earthly deprivation. The hungry shall be fed, the shoeless shod, the afflicted comforted, the persecuted exonerated. Though there are no signs that this restitution is forthcoming in the present, we are told to expect it in the future—a mythical future beyond death. With this expectation, the oppressed are persuaded to accept their condition of oppression, to live with deprivation rather than seek fulfillment here and now.

Marx sees this condition as one of alienation for the reason that persons are encouraged to remain passive in the face of an inexorable fate. They are made to believe there is nothing they can do to change their situation. That does not do credit to them as persons. For if there is anything that is characteristic of the person, it is his capacity to determine himself. By depriving persons of this capacity and investing it solely in God, religion subjects people to the worst sort of oppression. It deprives them of the freedom to be themselves.

The root cause of the problem for Marx was the social conditions of people, but it could also be seen as deriving from the sort of transcendence implicit in religious thought and action. It is a transcendence which places human good out of reach, takes it "out of this world" altogether. Attention is diverted from the real needs of people (food, shelter, clothing, meaningful work) and concentrated instead on remote and ethereal benefits which might eventually accrue to the person as a reward for his endurance. Furthermore, it is a transcendence in which the person is made to feel that he can do nothing about his future, that it is wholly "in the hands of God." He is thus provided with a rationale for his powerlessness and an inducement to acquiesce in the power exercised over him by others. This insures that whatever good does come to him will not be *his* doing. Transcendence of this sort is meaningless in the sense that it does not fully engage us as persons. It does not give significance to what we do.

Analytic philosophy has brought a quite different objection against the notion of transcendence. Out of a concern for language and a passion for clarity, a number of philosophers have come to the conclusion that the concept of God is basically unintelligible. It does not meet the requirements of coherent discourse. Thus, while it purports to say something about what is factually so, it does not admit of any sort of verification. There is no way of establishing conclusively whether God exists or not. How meaningful is it then even to speak of God? In other areas of knowledge we do not find it meaningful to speak of what cannot be proven one way or another. So why make an exception of religion?

But it is not only the non-verifiability of the concept of God which causes difficulty. It is also the seeming incoherence of the concept itself. Theologians speak of God as personal, as acting in certain definable ways and having characteristics commonly associated with persons (characteristics such as patience, wisdom, and love); yet at the same time they insist that he must be "omnipotent," "omniscient," and "eternal," a way of speaking which would seem to be in clear contradiction to this. How are we to reconcile two such diverse ways? What sense are we to make of a concept that is, to all appearances, internally contradictory? Surely anyone who stops to think about it is going to find this way of speaking fundamentally incoherent, and in that sense meaningless.

The problem once again is the transcendence implicit in religious discourse. It strains our ordinary ways of thinking and speaking. It obliges us to use words in ways which are at variance with ordinary usage—with the result that there is an appearance of meaning but no real meaning. The religious way of speaking fails even to make contact with the other ways of speaking. It operates in a world of its own. No wonder it has ceased to have much meaning for anyone.

If this seems like a highly theoretical account of the problem, consider how seldom it is that references of a traditionally religious sort are made in public anymore. It is as though they had ceased to have the meaning they once had, as though we no longer knew what to do with this way of speaking. More and more religion has become a purely private matter with meaning only for the person himself. But there is some question whether it can survive this sort of isolation and subjectification. There is the danger that whatever meaning remains will be further eroded by lack of contact with other ways of thinking, speaking, and feeling.

We began by saying that religion articulates a way of life. We seem to end up by saying that because of its transcendent reference it no longer makes contact with life. That would certainly be an ironic conclusion, but it may be one to which we are forced if we can find no acceptable understanding of transcendence.

MODELS AND IMAGES

The criticism that has been brought against the transcendent character of religion is a telling one. It exposes serious pitfalls to which religious language is susceptible, and therefore poses a serious challenge to anyone who would speak responsibly of God. It cannot simply be assumed that religious speech about God is meaningful. The possibility of an alien or empty concept of God is real: the evidence for both sorts of aberration is ample. Yet we may ask if this is the inevitable result of attempting to speak of what is "beyond" us. Must every attempt to give language a transcendent reference fall into one or another of these errors, or is there the possibility that religious discourse might retain its transcendent character and yet be meaningful?

Any but the most biased view of the history of ideas must acknowledge that religious thought has been profoundly influential. It has produced radical alterations in people's self-understanding and in their world view. It has affected the course of events and given to whole civilizations a pervasive and readily distinguishable character. One thinks, for instance, of the influence that Augustine's religious reflections have had on the shape of Western thought, or the continuing impress of Buddha's special type of spirituality on Eastern life and thought. Transcendence in such cases has not meant irrelevance or alienation. It has been an important way people have had of relating to their world.

So instead of looking upon secularity simply as a threat, we might rather consider it as a perspective from which to view religion and a stimulus for thinking critically about it. There have been times, after all, when religion so permeated a culture that it was difficult to get any kind of perspective on it. Then it was easy to confuse what is genuinely religious with what is only extraneously related to it. The sort of perspective which the secular context provides could, therefore, actually be a help in determining what it means to think and speak religiously. This is not to say that the secular viewpoint does not have its limitations when it comes to understanding religion, but only to suggest that it might also have a contribution to make.

If nothing more, the prevailing mood of secularity has had the effect of bringing to the fore the aspect of transcendence in religion. But now supposing we wanted to get some clarity on the subject of transcendence, how would we go about it? The language of religion is so diverse; it contains such a plethora of metaphors, images, concepts, and ideas that we scarcely know where to begin. In fact, one of the difficulties of the present situation as far as religion is concerned is that there is such a plurality of alternatives to choose from. Even within the Christian tradition there is great variety; but in addition there are other religions to consider. The likelihood of a single approach taking in all of the possibilities seems remote. Besides the very notion of transcendence is elusive to the point of being practically unintelligible. It may be unreasonable to suppose that we can achieve any sort of clarity on the subject. Still we ought to make the attempt. We ought to explore whatever sense there is to this way of speaking.

The way in which I propose to go about it is by considering various models of transcendence. This is an approach which has received some attention in recent years.[4] It is a variation on the earlier method of analogy, though obviously influenced by discussions of models in the natural and social sciences. Hopefully it can provide a way through the mass of detail which makes up a religious system. It may even provide a way of comparing systems. But most important of all, it should help us to get clear about what it means to speak of the transcendent. For that is the crux of our problem: we do not know what to make of this strange and elusive way of speaking.

4. There is a growing literature on this subject, but some of the most important items are as follows: Ian Barbour, *Myths, Models, and Paradigms* (New York: Harper & Row, 1973); Frederick Ferré, "Metaphors, Models, and Religion," *Soundings*, vol. 51, no. 3 (Fall 1968); Gordon Kaufman, "Two Models of Transcendence," *The Heritage of Christian Thought*, ed. R. E. Cushman and E. Grislis (New York: Harper & Row, 1965) and "On the Meaning of 'God': Transcendence without Mythology," *Harvard Theological Review*, vol. 59 (1966); Michael McLain, "On Theological Models," *Harvard Theological Review*, vol. 62 (1969); Ian Ramsey, *Models and Mystery* (New York: Oxford University Press, 1964).

Before considering possible models of transcendence, however, we ought to say something about models in general. In the natural sciences, a clear case of the use of a model is the linear theory of light, the conception of light traveling in a straight line.[5] It is a picture of sorts, but primarily it is a way of regarding something elusive and difficult to describe, a way of talking about it which enables us to understand it better. Thus, instead of thinking of light as simply "given," we think of it as proceeding in a direct line from source to object unless intercepted or otherwise interfered with. That is a less poetic way of regarding the phenomenon of light than some other ways, but also more explanatory in the sense that it permits us to make mathematical inferences we could not make otherwise. Given the height of an object and the angle of incidence, we can predict the length of shadow that will be cast by a particular source of light. If this seems obvious, it is only because the model is so widely accepted that it is taken for granted. That is also how it is with certain theological models: they are so deeply ingrained in our thinking that we are scarcely aware of their presence. Yet even a modicum of exposure to another culture soon convinces us that there are other ways of conceiving of the transcendent, other models for God than our own.

But at least when we speak of light we are speaking of something ostensively identifiable. We do not require a model to make us aware of the presence of light, as we do the presence of God. The role of the model in eliciting awareness of something that cannot be directly observed is more in evidence in the social and behavioral sciences. An example would be Freud's repression-transference theory.[6] It involves a kind of hydraulic model—pressures building up within a person and then being rechanneled, motivations appropriate to one situation coming to expression in another. Neither process is actually observable, yet the model provides a way of making sense of behavior which might otherwise seem meaningless and irrational. It enables us to "see" what the person is up to when he behaves in ways that are seemingly inappropriate. Freud's model does not lend itself to mathematical inference in the way that models in the natural sciences do, yet in the context of therapy it has proven to be quite useful. It has provided

5. Stephen Toulmin, *The Philosophy of Science* (London: Hutchinson's University Library, 1967), pp. 29 ff.

6. See, for example, A. C. MacIntyre, *The Unconscious: A Conceptual Analysis* (New York: Humanities Press, 1958).

insight into the behavior of persons that would not otherwise have been possible.

That is somewhat the way it is in religion. Terms such as sin, grace, salvation, enlightenment do not describe processes that can be directly observed, yet they do purport to speak of what is actually going on. They say what certain events mean in relation to the transcendent. This sort of meaning is obviously going to be much more elusive than anything to be found in the natural or social sciences. Verification procedures appropriate to the sciences (even the behavioral sciences) cannot be expected to apply to religion. Nor for that matter is the same attitude appropriate. The "scientific" attitude of detachment and objectivity simply does not fit the subject matter of religion. Still the difference may not be so great that we cannot speak of a significant use of models in both cases.

Ian Ramsey, who has given more attention to this subject than almost anyone else, contends that the use of models in religion is not so different from their use elsewhere. What the model provides in any case is not a literal description but "a collection of distinctive, reliable, and easily specifiable techniques for talking about a universe which is ultimately mysterious."[7] What is distinctive about the religious model is its irreducibility, the impossibility of getting back of it to some more basic form of reference. Also, there is the necessity of qualifying the religious model so as to indicate its transcendent reference. There is no language specifically for God, and no way of speaking of God which is not subject to the qualification of ultimacy. Still the fact that we speak of God or the transcendent in terms borrowed from more familiar areas of discourse and that this sort of "transfer of meaning" from one context to another is not peculiar to religion should mean that it is not a way of speaking entirely without precedent. It is analogous to other ways of speaking.

Ramsey has placed us all in his debt by the care and insight with which he has attempted to delineate the relationship between religious models and models of other sorts; yet I wonder if he has not overextended the category of model within the field of religion. For it would seem that he is prepared to call almost any religious concept or image a model. He speaks, for instance, of various biblical terms for God,

7. Ramsey, *Models and Mystery*, p. 4. See also his discussion of models in an earlier book, *Religious Language: An Empirical Placing of Theological Phrases* (New York: Macmillan, 1963), pp. 55 ff., and a subsequent article, "Talking About God," reprinted in *Words About God*, ed. Ian Ramsey (New York: Harper & Row, 1971).

such as Father, Shepherd, Warrior, King, as models; yet he also says that the concept *I* is a particularly apt model for God and that *activity* may provide the best model of all.[8] Aside from the question how one would go about preferring one model over another, there is some doubt in my own mind as to whether these are all models in the same sense. The first group of terms (Father, Shepherd, etc.) would appear to be of a quite different order from the second. For myself I would prefer to speak of them as images and reserve the term *model* for more general notions such as self and action.

There are several ways in which a model might be distinguished from an image. The greater generality of a model is one way. A term like agent or self can encompass a host of images, including such familiar ones as the potter working his clay, the father caring for his children, the judge presiding over a trial, and the king issuing executive orders to his subjects. An image is more limited in its meaning and more closely tied to historical contingencies, such as the social structure and the means of production. The imagery of kingship is obviously going to mean more in an age of monarchy than at some other time, just as the notion of God as Shepherd has connotations for a pastoral society that it cannot have for an urban, industrial society. This is not to take away from the force or effectiveness of an image; the right image will often move people in ways that nothing else can. It is simply to distinguish models from images in terms of their relative inclusiveness.

A model is more general, and therefore more extensible than an image; but it is also more basic. It can serve as the organizing principle for a whole system of thought in a way that an image cannot. It can give coherence to a set of images that might otherwise appear disparate and unrelated. The biblical literature with its vast array of images and its over two thousand years of history could easily lack any sort of coherence whatever; yet it is generally recognized to have a certain basic unity. One reason for this might be that there is a dominant model of transcendence which encompasses and thereby unifies the various images and metaphors used to speak of God. The same might be said for the Eastern religions—Hinduism, Buddhism, and Taoism. Their distinctive tone and outlook, in spite of many obvious differences, suggest a common approach to the transcendent and possibly a

8. Ramsey, *Words About God*, pp. 203–10. Compare *Religious Language*, pp. 73, 127.

common conception of it. What gives these diverse traditions a certain "family resemblance" may very well be the dominance of a particular model of transcendence.

That brings us to a final consideration. If the model is to be regarded as more basic than the image, it ought to stand in a different relationship to what it expresses; it ought to be somehow constitutive of one's relationship to the transcendent. And that means it ought itself to have something of the element of transcendence about it. If we already have some notion of transcendence, then we may employ any number of different images to express it. But if not, our choice of images is going to seem rather arbitrary and we are going to lack the critical principle by which to decide not only which images to use but in what respect they are to apply. A model, if it is to be sharply differentiated from an image, should fulfill this role. It should provide us with our most direct and immediate access to the transcendent, and should serve as the interpretive principle for whatever we say about it.

Where are we to find such a model? In our own tradition the answer seems fairly clear: it is to be found in the concept of person or self. Biblical religion, for all its diverse images of God, is quite consistent in conceiving of God as a Self, as One who is personally related to us. This implies a certain analogy between God and ourselves. God, presumably, transcends us in ways not unlike the ways in which we transcend one another and the larger world around us. There are differences, to be sure; but then it is a model we are dealing with and not a literal representation. At least there are some similarities. In speaking of the transcendent, we are not speaking of something totally foreign to our experiences.

Ramsey, as I have noted, considers the concept *I* a particularly appropriate model for God. That is largely because he sees a logical affinity between the two concepts. Neither is strictly empirical in the sense of being subject to empirical verification. We cannot prove the existence of the self, any more than we can prove the existence of God. Yet neither concept is exactly irrelevant to our understanding of the world. It makes a difference, for instance, whether we look upon other persons as selves or merely as mechanisms: it affects how we treat them. Similarly it makes a difference whether we regard the world as God's creation or merely as brute fact—though the difference may be difficult to specify. Both the concept of God and the concept of self have an elusive quality which is hard to pin down. It is this elusiveness, however, which gives them their logical affinity—and this in turn is related to the element of transcendence inherent in both.

This is not to suggest that there is only one concept of the self or that the self is the only possible model for the transcendent. The personal mode of discourse has had its critics in religion as elsewhere; yet it has also enjoyed widespread support. One reason might be that it is in terms of our own transcendence that we are most directly and immediately related to whatever it is that transcends us. Obviously if we have no experience of transcendence in ourselves, we are not likely to speak of a transcendence beyond ourselves. Still there are different models of transcendence, and not all of them are personal. At this stage in the discussion we do not need to consider the relative merits of different models but simply get clear about the term *model.*

A model is a way we have of conceiving of something which would otherwise elude us, something which is in an important sense beyond us. To speak of this reality as transcendent is not yet to indicate in what respect it is beyond us. That will depend on what we take as our model of transcendence. Different models will represent the transcendent differently. Yet whatever our model it cannot provide us with a literal picture of the reality we are speaking of. A model is at best a symbolic representation of something that cannot be directly observed. In that sense it functions on the outer limits of our language.[9] What it articulates, though, may be absolutely central to our experience, the primary referent in our understanding of ourselves and our world. It is characteristic of a religious model that it has this kind of centrality however elusive the reality of which it speaks.

THEOLOGY AS GRAMMAR

The radical secularization of society over the last several hundred years—whatever the conditions which have produced it, and they are undoubtedly many—has resulted in a greater self-consciousness about religion than at any other time in history. Thus, even those who continue to think and speak "religiously" frequently do so with a certain unease. They are aware that this way of thinking does not quite fit in with the prevailing assumptions of the day and may even be inconsistent with their own basic attitudes. Do I really mean what I say when

9. Compare Paul van Buren, *The Edges of Language* (New York: Macmillan, 1972).

I speak in this way? Is there any real meaning to this way of speaking? Anyone who is at all reflective about his religion has surely asked himself these questions at one time or another. It is a measure of the secularity of our age that scarcely anyone can take his religion for granted any longer.

At the same time that this secularization process has been going on, there has been an increasing tendency on the part of philosophers to concentrate their attention upon language. The task of the philosopher has come to be seen not as one of providing us with information about the world—information that can only be obtained through speculation—but of furnishing insight into the various ways we have of talking about the world. The philosopher, in other words, deals in meanings: he helps us to make sense of what we are saying rather than gives us something new to say. That is a modest task compared with the more ambitious undertakings of the past; yet coming at this particular time it could be a great boon to religion. For if there was ever a time when the religious community needed help in understanding its language, its distinctive way of speaking, this is it.

In the early years of what has become to be known as analytical philosophy, it did not appear that it could offer much help to religion. If anything, it seemed to provide legitimation for the secularizing tendency in society. A. J. Ayer's *Language, Truth and Logic* is a classic of this genre.[10] He argues, in effect, that all religious assertions are meaningless because they fail to come up to the standard of scientific assertions. They are unverifiable; and since they are not merely tautological, they must be meaningless. It is not even correct to say that they are false, for that would imply that they had some meaning. What is meaningless can be neither asserted nor contradicted; it can only be repudiated as nonsensical. Talk about a transcendent God epitomizes for Ayer the sort of nonsense to be found in religion.

Others have taken a similar line so that analytical philosophy has become identified in many people's minds with the denial of religion. Yet this is not all there is to it. Even at the time that Ayer was publishing his broadside attack on religion, Ludwig Wittgenstein, whose earlier work *Tractatus Logico-Philosophicus* had helped to launch the movement, was beginning to reconsider his view of language along lines less prejudicial to religion. Whereas he had previ-

10. A. J. Ayer, *Language, Truth and Logic* (New York: Dover, 2d edition, 1946). See especially pp. 114–20.

ously thought that it was his task as a philosopher to distinguish what can from what cannot be said, he came increasingly to feel that everything is "in order as it is." So instead of laying down rules which an assertion must satisfy in order to be meaningful, he advises, in his later work entitled *Philosophical Investigations*, that we look at how words and sentences are used, the actual role they play in the life situation of people, and take that as our clue to their meaning.[11]

There are, he thought, an indefinite number of different uses to which language can be put: giving and obeying orders, describing an object, explaining an event, telling a story, asking, thanking, cursing, greeting, praying. Each of these uses is set within a "form of life" with its characteristic concerns and tacit assumptions. Where a way of speaking has an identifiable coherence, a recognizable order, he calls it a "language game."[12] This is a useful way of thinking about language for it makes us aware of just how much the meaning of individual words is dependent upon their total context. In order to know what is meant by a "queen," for instance, it is necessary to know what game is being played. Is it chess or bridge or politics? There is no abstract essence of "queenness" waiting to be discovered. Rather it is a matter of knowing what game is being played and what the role of the queen is in that game. It is much the same, Wittgenstein thinks, with the words in our language. Their meaning is largely determined by their use, which in turn is governed by the "rules of the game."

The job of the philosopher is not to make the rules but to discover them. His task is like that of a grammarian—a comparison which Wittgenstein himself makes.[13] He distinguishes, however, between what he calls "surface grammar" and "depth grammar." The former is what we ordinarily think of as grammar—the construction of a sentence, rules for different kinds of words, conventions of various sorts—whereas the latter has to do with the *sense* of what is said, the *logic* of a particular language game. The philosopher as grammarian must endeavor to distinguish different language games and make clear their differences. A great deal of misunderstanding can result simply from confusing one language game with another or mistaking the actual character of a particular language game. It might be supposed, for

11. Wittgenstein, *Philosophical Investigations*, pars. 98, 124, 340.
12. Ibid., pars. 7, 23.
13. Ibid., pars. 660, 664.

instance, that talking about a pain is like talking about a color sensation, when in fact the two ways of speaking are quite different. Similarly religion is sometimes confused with science or morals. Without attempting to justify a particular language game, a philosopher can perform a useful service simply by describing and analyzing it.

This is the primary direction in which philosophy has gone in recent years. It has been principally concerned with the analysis of concepts and the mapping of relationships between different conceptual schemes. In the process some attention has been given to religious language, but generally by those whose primary commitments are elsewhere. What has been especially lacking is any serious attempt to deploy the technique of analysis in the service of systematic theology. Wittgenstein, in one of his more cryptic passages in the *Investigations*, suggests that it might be the role of the theologian to do just that—perhaps he too should think of himself as a "grammarian."[14]

Does this mean that the theologian ought to leave everything as it is, that he ought to do nothing to unsettle or revise our thinking about God or the transcendent? Not necessarily, for Wittgenstein himself did not leave everything as it was. Through his analysis he provided a fresh perception of language and showed a way through many of the difficulties that beset us in our use of words. That surely is one way of changing things! Besides even if we go on saying many of the same things that we have in the past, the meaning will not necessarily be the same. In fact, it is almost certain to change as we subject it to analysis. Simply by mapping a familiar terrain, we make it different: it is no longer quite what it was. But that is not all. We may as a result of analysis conclude that there are some things we will not want to say which we are now saying, and other things we will need to say which we are not now saying, if we are to remain true to the underlying sense of our tradition. Analysis by itself cannot decide such questions, but it can help to clear the way for a decision.

In the discussion which follows I intend to deal with substantive issues of the Christian tradition. I do not propose simply to summarize different theories of meaning or to catalog various uses of the word *God.* Instead I want to use analysis as a tool to get at the conceptual foundations of our religious way of speaking in order thereby to criticize and revise it. In other areas where analysis has been carried out

14. Ibid., par. 373.

with rigor and persistence, it has led to a fresh perception and solution of long-standing issues. One thinks, for instance, of Gilbert Ryle's critique of the Cartesian concept of mind as something wholly private and inaccessible to others, and more recently the Wittgensteinian critique of behaviorism with its mechanistic conception of persons and their action. There is no reason why analysis in the area of religion could not fulfill a similar constructive role. We will need to know, however, what we intend to do with it. What I propose to do is, first, to analyze certain basic models of transcendence, and then to see what can meaningfully be said of God with the aid of these models.

The models I will be considering are all taken from the sphere of the personal. That is to say, they will have to do with our sense of personal identity. In part this is because it is a characteristic feature of our religious tradition to speak of God in personal terms; there are exceptions, to be sure, but in the main Christians have adhered rather closely to a personal conception of God—and if we mean to stay within our tradition we must reckon with this characteristic way of speaking. But it is also because of the greater accessibility of the transcendent approached in this way. Supposing, for instance, we took as our model some relationship observed in nature. It might be a causal relationship, such as obtains between an event and its antecedent condition, or an organic relationship, such as a plant has to its environment. The difficulty with such models is that they are largely external to us; we have little or no intrinsic understanding of the relationships involved. A personal model, on the other hand, is intrinsic: it implies personal involvement. That could be a very important factor not only in determining the intelligibility of the concept of God but in assessing its personal relevance. If this way of speaking is to be meaningful in more than a formal sense, it must somehow relate back to ourselves—and what better way of insuring that it does than by beginning with the self?

There are, however, different ways of conceiving of the self; so even if we stay within the personalistic tradition there is the possibility of conceiving of God in more than one way. And that is probably a good thing, for it means that we have some critical perspective on our own tradition. We are not locked into a particular way of thinking with no recourse except to abandon the tradition altogether. In fact, what I am proposing to do can in a way be regarded as *an internal critique of the personalistic tradition in theology*. Simply because this way of speaking about God has encountered difficulties in the modern period need not mean that it should be given up. It may be that we should first rethink our concept of the person. This could make a very great difference for our understanding of God.

If it is still objected that commitment to a particular religious tradition is too restrictive, I can only reply that I have not found it so. On the contrary, I would say that commitment to some tradition or other is indispensable to understanding what religion is all about. For without some such commitment, the language of religion is liable to seem lifeless and abstract. The subject matter is elusive enough without divorcing it from its setting in a particular community. Even where this is attempted, it is doubtful whether it is ever fully carried out. For invariably there is a "hidden agenda," an unacknowledged religious tradition forming one's concept of religion and affecting one's judgment about it.[15]

Let us be clear then that we are coming at this question of meaning from within a particular religious tradition, a tradition whose characteristic way of speaking of the transcendent is personal. We are not considering just any concept of God, but rather one that has had a dominant influence on Western thought over the ages. If anything, it is too familiar. It is difficult to get a critical perspective on it. Yet this perspective can be had if we will first get clear about the different models of personal transcendence. From considering what it might mean to speak of the self as transcendent, we should have a better idea of what it would mean to speak of God in this way.

But then where shall we go for an analysis of this way of speaking? Who will instruct us in the various models of self-identity? No doubt there are many possibilities. Psychologists, sociologists, and philosophers of various persuasions have dealt with this question in recent times, and some of their ideas are quite significant. Yet the approach which is most congruent with a concern for language is that taken by the analytical philosophers—particularly those influenced in one way or another by the later Wittgenstein. They have compiled a considerable body of literature over the past twenty-five years dealing with personal concepts, such as thought and action, emotion and will, self-identity and bodily identity. This field of inquiry has even gained a special title: the philosophy of mind. The most prominent thinkers

15. This would seem to be the case with Langdon Gilkey's *Naming the Whirlwind: The Renewal of God-Language* (Indianapolis: Bobbs-Merrill, 1969).

associated with the philosophy of mind (in addition to Wittgenstein) include Gilbert Ryle, J. L. Austin, P. F. Strawson, Elizabeth Anscombe, Peter Geach, Norman Malcolm, and John Wisdom—but there are many others as well. The whole field is a rich mine of insights waiting to be worked.

Over a century ago, Friedrich Schleiermacher began his classic work, *The Christian Faith*, with what he called "propositions borrowed from ethics," by which he meant propositions having to do with the concept of self.[16] I believe he was on the right track, except that I would speak of propositions borrowed from the philosophy of mind. At a time when there is confusion as to the meaning of religious concepts, notably the concept of God, I believe we would benefit from an analysis of related concepts having to do with the self. It is not that the two ways of speaking are identical but that they are related. Analysis of the one should aid our understanding of the other—if only by providing us with a meaningful frame of reference.

Chapters 2 and 3 will be given over to this preliminary analysis, in which our objective will be to lay a groundwork for the theological argument that is to follow. In these chapters we will use various philosophical writings. Our purpose will not be to give a comprehensive account of the thought of any one man, but to set forth some possible models of transcendence so that when we turn our attention to the meaning of God we will have a critical perspective from which to work. Insofar as philosophical analysis can aid us in this task, we will make use of it; insofar as it cannot, we will ignore it. There is certainly no suggestion that the philosophers we are appealing to are themselves theologians (even crypto-theologians). For the most part they are not, and there is no reason they should be. For our purposes it is enough that they have said some true and illuminating things about the self.

Chapters 4, 5, and 6 will concentrate on the theological argument, beginning with the concept of God. The first question to be considered is whether it is possible on the basis of various models of transcendence to speak intelligibly of God. Are the qualifications which must

16. Friedrich Schleiermacher, *The Christian Faith* (New York: Harper & Row, 1963), secs. 3–6. His analysis of the self takes various forms, including the distinction between knowing, doing, and feeling, relative states of dependence and freedom, and varying degrees of self-consciousness. These distinctions help to place religion, but are not derived from it. They are, in other words, defensible independently of religious considerations.

be made in order to give language this kind of reference such as to render it meaningless, or is it a legitimate extension of meaning to speak in this way? The concepts we use are going to be stretched in any case; the question is whether they are stretched beyond the breaking point. Do we really know what we are talking about when we speak of a transcendent Self?

But supposing we do; even if the concept is coherent we may still have a problem identifying the referent. It may be meaningless in a more practical sense. This is where our reliance on a particular religious tradition becomes evident. For it is by reference to Christ that the concept of God takes on definiteness and particularity—at least for the Christian. Christ is the embodiment of God's intention for us: the decisive event in which God has declared himself to us. The skeptic may wonder if this claim is really true or not, but our concern will be limited to a determination of whether it is *meaningful* or not.

Finally, though, we shall want to consider how this way of speaking bears on our self-understanding and our world view. What are its *personal* implications? Is it "alienating" as the Marxists say it is, or "vacuous" as some of the analysts maintain? Given the secular context within which theology must be carried out in this day, these are the sorts of questions which cannot be ignored. In fact, for most people this is where the question of meaning really becomes crucial. Other considerations, such as conceptual coherence, may seem by comparison rather academic. Yet without some conceptual scheme in which to place it, the more personal question of meaning is liable not even to arise. Certainly it is going to be more difficult to handle without a frame of reference of some kind. We begin, therefore, with the larger conceptual issues, though eventually we mean to correlate our theoretical models with actual patterns of religious life.

To recapitulate, we want to get clear about what it might *mean* to speak of God in a context both secular and Christian. This is a multileveled undertaking, yet theological throughout. If it seems like a rather unusual way of doing theology, it may nevertheless be a necessary way in a time of acute linguistic self-consciousness and general religious uncertainty.

2. MODELS OF TRANSCENDENCE

To speak of God we must be able to speak of what transcends us. If we consider *any* transcendent reference meaningless, we are not going to find much meaning in the concept of God. For God epitomizes what is transcendent. If, however, we remain open to the possibility of transcendence, even while remaining skeptical of specific claims concerning the transcendent, we will be in a position to consider what form transcendence might take and thence what it might mean to speak of God.

But how shall we begin? There is no clear or easy way of approaching the subject of transcendence. Certainly there is no one way; the great diversity among religions is evidence of that. Men have followed many different routes in their quest for the transcendent. If we begin with the self, as we have determined to do, it is because of its relative accessibility and because it seems to have the character of transcendence. Intuitively the self is not fully a part of the world; it stands somehow outside of things.

Besides, there is a need eventually to relate what we say about God back to ourselves. If it is to be personally meaningful, this way of speaking must have some bearing on our own self-understanding. So we might as well begin there. If the self can provide the basic model for transcendence, we would do well to make use of it. This may create other problems (anthropomorphism, for instance), but we face these when we come to them.

ELUSIVE SUBJECT

Many philosophers and theologians have noted similarities between the word *I* and the word *God*. Ian Ramsey speaks of them as having a similar "logic." Rudolph Bultmann says that they both refer to matters beyond the visible world and are therefore incapable of proof. Paul Tillich speaks of discovering oneself in discovering God. In all of these ways of speaking, there is a general recognition that God and self are analogous concepts with analogous roles to play in our language. It should not be unusual then if the one should serve as the model for the other, if in order to get clear about the concept of God we should look to the concept of self.

But this assumes that we know what it means to refer to the self. That is an assumption that can be challenged. We certainly use the word *I* as if we knew what we were talking about; but if we were asked to explain what we mean by it we would probably be hard pressed to give a satisfactory answer, for it is in many ways a very puzzling idea. There is, for instance, the fact that everyone uses it to refer to someone different. I use it to refer to myself; you use it to refer to yourself. The reference is continually changing. There is also the non-verifiability of many typical "I" statements. If someone says he is feeling a certain way or thinking certain thoughts, there is not much we can say to dispute him. His use of the word *I* gives an authority to what he says that second- or third-person statements seem to lack. Then, too, there is the immediacy and certainty with which we refer to ourselves. As Descartes noted long ago, I can doubt almost anything but myself as the subject doing the doubting. Still when it comes to identifying this subject, we are generally at a loss. There is no easy way to get this self of which we are so certain into view.

Let us therefore begin by considering what it might mean to speak of the self. It is in the first place a reflexive way of speaking. The word *I* refers back to the speaker or, in the case of action, to the agent. It is not like picking out an object from a range of alternatives, or even like naming an object. The fact that everyone uses this same word *I* to identify himself means that it is probably more ostensive than it is descriptive. But even if you think of it as a kind of verbal pointing, it is an odd sort where the pointer is that which is pointed to. It is rather like trying to point at the finger doing the pointing. It would seem to be an impossibility, yet in the case of the self it is done.

We could simplify the problem greatly by saying that the word *I* refers to a particular body, namely, *my* body. But that would be to beg the question, for how do we get the notion of something being *mine* except by implicit use of the concept *I*? Besides, when I refer to myself I do not have to first observe myself, as it would seem that I should if the reference of the word *I* were simply to a particular body. Some philosophers and novelists have even speculated about the possibility of bodily exchange between persons. And in an age of transplants it is not inconceivable that I might assume a different body, yet remain the same self. All of which goes to show that self-identity cannot be simply reduced to bodily identity.

In what then does it consist? If self-reference is not bodily reference, perhaps it is a purely subjective form of reference. When I use the word *I*, I identify myself as a subject, as a center of consciousness, as one who has objects in view but is not itself an object. Thus when I refer to myself I make explicit the subjectivity implicit in every statement I make. Whether I am talking about ideas or persons, natural events or social processes, cabbages or kings, my own subjectivity is involved. I am the one doing the talking; what I observe I observe from my own particular vantage point; the interpretation of what I see, feel, and do is my own. This subjectivity which accompanies every statement I make is irreducible.

It is also quite elusive, since every attempt to get it into view invariably makes an object out of it. Thus, while I can in a sense observe myself, I cannot observe myself as the observer. Retrospectively I may take into consideration my own past behavior, much as I might the behavior of another, yet I cannot include the one doing the considering in the consideration. Looking "within"—attending to one's thoughts, feelings, impressions—does nothing to alter this basic situation. For it is still the one doing the looking that is sought. The self as subject seems to be always "behind" us, presupposed rather than objectively known. The self as subject is systematically elusive.

Wittgenstein in his early philosophical writing touches on this question of the elusiveness of the self and concludes that the self is not, properly speaking, a part of the world. The self as subject is like the eye as seer. Just as the eye is not a part of the visual field, the self is not a part of its world. It is rather a "limit" of the world. It is what makes this world *my* world.[1] The self as subject cannot be included in an objective account of the world, yet it is implicit in any account I might give of the world. For such an account would be my account; it would presuppose my unique perspective on the world.

The Dutch philosopher Van Peursen expresses this view quite eloquently when he writes that "the 'I' is a central reality" in everyday experience. It is "the inalienable viewpoint which cannot be swapped for that of anybody else." It means that "the whole of life assumes a

1. Ludwig Wittgenstein, *Tractatus Logico-Philosophicus* (New York: Humanities Press, 1961), 5.632–5.641.

constant perspective, from myself outwards, and that the totality of world is what it is experientially for me."[2] So basic is this I-perspective that a person will defend it against every incursion. Not only physical threat to displace me from my position in the world, but logical threats as well are instinctively rejected. Thus, a purely mechanistic account of the world in which no provision is made for a person's perspective on the world may elicit a hostile, defensive reaction. It may be seen as a denial of self, and therefore as a threat to myself, every bit as much as a physical assault. If a person identifies with his perspective on the world, he is not going to take lightly to its denial.

But then is this all that can be said about the self as subject, that it constitutes a perspective on the world? It would seem that anything else we say is going to be of a basically negative sort. The self is not a part of its world. It is not available for observation or description—at least not in the usual sense of the term. Its presence or absence cannot be publicly verified. The certainty we have concerning the self is of an essentially private, subjective sort. That does not make it any less real or significant, but it does put it in a different category from matters which are public and open to observation and it limits what can be said about it.

This brings us back to the question of transcendence. One reason that the self as model has great appeal to thinkers such as Ramsey is that it seems to be in line with the traditional idea of God. For God, too, is not a part of the world. He is not a being that can be observed, described, or pointed to. If he is within our experience at all, it is in a way that is elusive and difficult to grasp. Some have even claimed that the way to know God is the way in which the self is known, that is to say, reflexively. By knowing oneself "in depth" one comes to know God. The model of the elusive self, therefore, commends itself as a theological model both on conceptual grounds and on grounds of religious experience.

Yet it is not without its difficulties. For one thing, it is terribly abstract. Once you have distinguished the self from the world, what is there that you can say about it? The elusive "I" may be implicated in everything we think and do and feel, yet it is not something that can itself be thought about, acted upon, or felt. Its presuppositional status makes it very difficult to get into view. Just because it is so elusive it

2. C. A. Van Peursen, *Body, Soul, Spirit: A Survey of the Body-Mind Problem* (New York: Oxford University Press, 1966), p. 8.

can scarcely be thought. How then is it going to assist us in our search for a greater transcendence? Can that which is itself scarcely intelligible provide the key to a greater mystery?

In a negative way, perhaps it can. If the self is conceivable as somehow distinct from the world, God may be also. Anyway the sort of reductionism that brings everything down to the level of observation and verification is excluded. So long as there is transcendence within oneself, there is the possibility of transcendence beyond oneself. Yet one might wish for something more positive than this.

It is doubtful though whether it can be had with this model. For presumably anything we say must be nonobjective. Insofar as our model of transcendence is the self as subject, there is no way in which we can speak of God except as Subject—without forfeiting his transcendence. So either we confine ourselves to a negative mode of discourse or we keep silent. Those would seem to be the only alternatives.

Rudolph Bultmann provides a possible solution to this dilemma in his "existential" interpretation of transcendence.[3] He is highly critical of all objectifying interpretations of God. He considers them "mythological" and therefore unacceptable on both rational and religious grounds. Yet he is not prepared to abandon all talk about God. He retains, for instance, the notion of the "action of God," so long as it is understood that it is not something objectively describable. But then what sort of meaning can it have?

The concept of transcendence, he contends, would have an exclusively negative meaning were it not for its existential implications. Because in speaking of God I also speak of myself—and not in some general sense but in a highly personal, immediate sense—it is possible to give a positive meaning to statements about God. Talk about the action of God, for instance, is a way of indicating the transcendent basis of a radically new life. The "word of God" calls man to God, but at the same time bestows upon him a new self-understanding. By speaking of oneself in a particular way, it is possible to speak indirectly of God.

In this way Bultmann holds on to the model of elusive subjectivity and still manages to say something positive. He does so by speaking reflexively both about God and the self. Yet is it possible by this method to distinguish God and the self? What becomes of the "other-

3. See especially Rudolph Bultmann, *Jesus Christ and Mythology* (New York: Charles Scribner's Sons, 1958).

ness" of God? Bultmann is not unaware of this difficulty but tends to dismiss it by appeal to a vague notion of encounter. Faith arises out of encounter, and encounter implies an Other. We can speak of this encounter, though, only in terms of its effect upon us. So the solution is still basically reflexive: theological concepts derive their meaning from their existential implications.

This is an important way of approaching the subject of transcendence and deserves to be taken seriously in spite of the objections that can be brought against it. The wide appeal of Bultmann's existential interpretation of theology is testimony to the force of this particular model. Intuitively we do sense an affinity between our own elusive subjectivity and the transcendence of God. Yet if we do not wish to slip into a pious agnosticism when it comes to speaking of God, it may be necessary to supplement this model with another of a more objective sort.

SELF-IN-COMMUNITY

Starting with the elusive "I" gives one an immediate transcendence of the world. The subject, as Wittgenstein says, is not a part of the world. Yet this transcendence is purchased at a price, namely the isolation of the self from others. For if the self is not a part of the world, if it eludes every objectification, how could I ever know any self other than my own? Where the only access to the self is reflexive, the only self that can be known is one's own self. But this means that if God is to be thought of as a self one is in the awkward position of either not being able to identify God or being unable to distinguish God from oneself. On the model of the elusive subject, God is either unknowable or an aspect of oneself.

Theologically this is a difficult position to accept for it would seem to be indistinguishable from agnosticism. But theological considerations aside, it does not properly represent our actual experience of others. For it is simply not the case that the only self I know is my own self. Whenever I listen to someone talk and take in his meaning I have access to his subjectivity. He is a part of my world; yet he is also a subject in his own right. And though I do not enter into his subjectivity to such an extent that his world becomes my world, nevertheless, he is subject for me. He is not simply an object like any other object.

The standard reply to this objection would be that while I do not have immediate access to another's subjectivity, I can at least infer from his behavior that he is a subject like myself. I observe, for instance, that whenever I have certain intentions, such as the intention to raise my arm, my body behaves in a certain way (in this case, my arm goes up.) Therefore, when I observe a similar movement in others, I infer a similar intention. I analogize from my own case. I conclude that if others can do what I do they must be subjects like me. They must be transcendently related to their world as I am to mine.

This account of intersubjective experience has a certain plausibility, for we all have had the experience of being puzzled by someone else's behavior and attempting to understand it by way of our own. I see someone doing something odd and I think, "Now if that were me, what would I be up to?" Yet this is hardly the normal way in which we arrive at someone else's intentions. Ordinarily I can "see" what a person is up to simply by observing his behavior. No inference is necessary—much less an inference that refers back to myself. The other person's behavior exhibits a certain pattern or meaning and I assume this to be the meaning he intends it to have. If I had to stop every time and think, "What would I be intending if I were to behave in that way?" interpersonal relations would be even more awkward and painful than they now are. Besides, when I do analogize about another person's behavior, it is seldom by way of self-observation; more commonly it is by putting myself imaginatively in his place and seeing things from his perspective as much as possible.

Yet apart from the fact that this account of our way of understanding others does not seem to be in accord with ordinary experience, there are conceptual difficulties. One of the most telling arguments against it, in fact, is to be found in Wittgenstein's own later writings in which he subjects some of his earlier views to criticism. I am thinking in particular of his argument against "private language."[4] A private language is not a language which happens to be meaningful to only one person—it is not at all difficult to imagine someone setting up his own private code. Rather what is meant is a language, a way of speaking, which is in principle intelligible only to the person using it. References to pain, for instance, might be thought to be meaningful only to the person feeling the pain. "How can anyone else know what I'm talking about when I talk about *my* pain? They can't feel what I'm feeling." This sort of claim would seem to be a variation on what

4. Ludwig Wittgenstein, *Philosophical Investigations* (New York: Macmillan, 1953), pars. 295, 243, 258–259. See also Norman Malcolm, "Wittgenstein's *Philosophical Investigations*," *The Philosophical Review*, vol. 43 (1954), pp. 530–59.

we were earlier saying about the elusive "I." The word *I* is reflexive; it identifies a point of view which no one else shares; so how can it mean anything to anyone else? The most that a person can do, it would seem, is to appeal to his own use of "I" and hope that it bears some relation to the other person's use.

But if this were so, how would we ever have learned to use self-referential language in the first place? Who would have taught us to speak in this way or corrected us when we were found to be misusing basic concepts? Language is fundamentally social. It is the medium of communication between persons. The way we learn to use words is from others. This is as true for subjective references as for objective references. Thus, the way in which a person learns to speak about his feelings is by having someone observe his behavior and tell him what he is feeling. A child falls and scrapes his knee and begins to cry. His mother sees what has happened and says to him, "Your knee hurts. Let me put some medicine on it. That will make it feel better." She does not need to feel what he is feeling to know that he is in pain or to teach him the word for pain. His behavior suffices to indicate that he is in pain. Moreover, as the child grows more adept in the use of language, he will learn to substitute words for behavior in identifying his pain to others. He will say, "My knee hurts," rather than simply cry out in anguish.

Does this mean then that we have to observe our own behavior to know that we are in pain? Of course not. The person that is in pain knows that he is in pain because of how he feels. He would not, however, know to call what he was feeling "pain" were it not that the behavior of persons suffices to identify them as in pain. In order for words to be meaningful, we must have some way of explaining them to others and that in turn requires that they have some other reference than to what is known only to the person himself. A meaning that was exclusively private would have no place in the language and therefore would not really qualify as a meaning.

What Wittgenstein is objecting to, as he makes clear at one point, is a certain picture we have of ourselves. It is summed up in the proposition, "I know . . . only from my own case." It is a picture which represents the person as basically isolated from others, shut up in his own subjectivity. He can observe the behavior of others, but in order to know what it means in a personal sense he must refer back to himself. There is, in other words, a fundamental hiatus between self and others. The more that we focus upon the uniqueness and inalienability of the "I," the more likely we are to evoke this picture. Yet it represents a distortion of the way in which we use language, which is primarily within a social context. The self is distinct, but distinct in relation to other selves. First- and third-person assertions belong together; they ought not be separated or reduced to one or the other. In the "grammar" of self-identification each is indispensable to the other.

P. F. Strawson makes a similar point in a more formal way in his article, "Persons."[5] He maintains that it is one of the distinguishing characteristics of "personal predicates" that they should be ascribed to others on the basis of observation and to oneself apart from observation. "To learn their use is to learn both aspects of their use."[6] He gives the example of the person who is depressed. We may speak of him behaving in a depressed way and also of his feeling depressed. One might suppose that the depression he feels is one thing and the depression we observe is another, but in fact the concept of depression encompasses both uses. It belongs to the structure of our language that it should have both uses and that there should be no difference of meaning in the two uses.

What is it that bridges the gap between self and others? For Strawson, it is the bodiliness of the person. I would have no way of identifying another subject of experience were he not a bodily subject; yet without the possibility of referring to others self-reference would be meaningless. "The main point here is a purely logical one: the idea of a predicate is correlative with that of a range of distinguishable individuals of which the predicate can be significantly, though not necessarily truly, affirmed."[7] So in order to refer meaningfully to oneself as subject, one must be able to refer to others as subjects; and that in turn is dependent upon their being bodily subjects, observably identifiable subjects. There might be some use for the concept of pure subjectivity, but it would have to be a secondary use. The concept of the person as a bodily subject is "logically primitive."

Because of the bodiliness of the person, the word *I* is not simply a

5. P. F. Strawson, "Persons," *Minnesota Studies in the Philosophy of Science* (Minneapolis: University of Minnesota Press, 1958). The same article appears as chapter three in Strawson's *Individuals: An Essay in Descriptive Metaphysics* (London: Methuen, 1961). A paperback edition of *Individuals* was published in America by Doubleday in 1963; page references to this edition will be placed in brackets following references to the original.

6. Ibid., p. 108 [105].

7. Ibid., p. 99 n. [95 n.].

private point of reference; it is public as well. As a bodily self, I am aware of other bodily selves. Indeed, if what certain sociologists say is correct, my self-awareness is dependent on my awareness of others and their awareness of me. I form my self-concept largely in terms of how others perceive me. The child, for instance, gets his initial idea of himself from the way in which his parents respond to him. Later on others may take the place of the parent in providing him with an objective view of himself. It may even be an idealized other which fulfills this role for him. Yet without some "significant other" to confirm who he is, the person is likely to have a very weak sense of self.

Conversely, though, the body cannot be simply an object to others. The person must be perceived as a bodily subject and treated accordingly. If the person is only regarded as a thing, he will be unable to form an adequate concept of himself as subject. He will have a tendency to disassociate from his body and treat it as a thing, thus preserving his subjectivity but at a very great price. The concept of person is a holistic concept, encompassing both objective and subjective factors—and should be so regarded by the person himself as well as others.

Briefly stated, the bodily self is a social self, inextricably related to others. Self-knowledge on this model incorporates knowledge of others. Another's point of view is not intrinsically alien to my own or ultimately inaccessible to me as a subject. To be sure, the viewpoint of another remains *his* viewpoint. I do not actually become the other person. Nevertheless, I do have access to his way of thinking; I have the possibility of sharing his viewpoint, and therefore of seeing myself as he sees me. That constitutes a kind of transcendence.

But does it really get me beyond the limitations of my individuality? I may be able to correct for some of my own biases through exposure to the biases of others, but that hardly adds up to a universal point of view. If I mean fundamentally to transcend the relativities of my situation, I will need to do more than simply exchange one relative viewpoint for another. I will need a form of transcendence that is in principle universalizable. Such is to be found in the notion of community. For when I join a community, I do not simply take on the perspective of another individual; I assume a point of view that transcends both my own and that of other individuals. The community, insofar as it is a community and not simply an amalgam of individuals, has its own distinct identity, a more inclusive identity than is possible for even the most empathetic individual.

If the key word for the mode of transcendence we have been considering up till now is the word *I*, the key word for this particular form of transcendence is *we*. A "we" identity has some of the same elusiveness as an "I" identity in that it is not reducible to an observable state of affairs, yet it is not purely subjective or inaccessible to others. It is by definition a shared identity. In addition, there is a greater possibility of universality than with the more subjective approach. Communities may be quite narrow in outlook, but they have a capacity for inclusiveness greater than that of the individual. There is really no limit to the possible scope of a communal identity.

One of the most penetrating analyses of this particular model of transcendence is to be found in the writings of Josiah Royce, an early twentieth-century American philosopher.[8] He argues that the community represents a distinctly different "level" of human life from the individual. It is not simply an aggregate of individuals. It includes individuals but also transcends them by incorporating them into a more inclusive whole. The individual who participates in a community finds his identity enhanced; without ceasing to be an individual, he becomes more than an individual; he enters a life "incomparably vaster" than anything he has previously known.

But what is it that gives the community its identity? If it is not simply an aggregate of individuals, it must have some principle of unity that holds it together. Here is where Royce's analysis is most incisive. He first considers the existence of the community through time and concludes that the community, like the individual, derives its sense of identity in large part from a remembered past and an anticipated future. Neither the individual self nor the community is a "mere present datum, or collection of data." A community constituted primarily by the identification of its members with a particular past would be a "community of memory"; a community united around the expectation of some future event would be a "community of hope."

Yet it is not simply the relationship of individual selves to a common past or a common future that makes them a community; it is also their allegiance to a common cause. For Royce this is the overriding consideration. Loyalty to a cause, more than anything else, is what binds a group of individuals together and makes of them a community. The causes for which men unite are various, but the "spirit of loyalty" is essentially the same. It is what enables men to transcend

8. See especially Josiah Royce, *The Problem of Christianity* (Chicago: University of Chicago Press, 1968), pp. 75–98, 229–71.

their individual differences, to overcome conflicts of interest, and to work together for a common good. The ultimate outcome of such loyalty, he feels, will be a "universal community of the loyal," for only in such a community can the ideal of loyalty be fully realized. "To this community in ideal all men belong; and to act as if one were a member of such a community is to win in the highest measure the goal of individual life. It is to win what religion calls salvation."[9]

What we have here, then, is a notion of social transcendence clearly distinguishable from individual transcendence. It is not that the self is given up, but that the self-other dichotomy so characteristic of individual transcendence is overcome. When I join with others in a common cause, I am no longer an "I" solely by distinction from others; I have my identity in common with others. I am a self-in-community. Royce is surely right to speak of this as a different level of human life, and not simply as an enlargement of individual self-interest. What passes for social transcendence may be no more than self-interest writ large, but then we do not have true community. The true community is one that is at least in principle universal.

There is some question, though, whether the sort of transcendence represented by this model suits our purpose. Can it serve as a theological model? Royce argues that it can, pointing out that it has played an important role in shaping the Christian consciousness. Both the Pauline concept of the church as the "body of Christ" and Jesus' own teaching concerning the Kingdom of God incorporate this model. Salvation is not thought of as a strictly individual affair but as involving the person in his relations with others. To enter into relationship with God is to be taken up into an inclusive fellowship with others. It is to belong to that "ideal community" only faintly suggested by the many lesser communities (family, school, nation, church) to which we give our loyalty.

But does this make it a model for God? Surely we are not to equate God and the community. That would be a solution of sorts, but one with highly pantheistic overtones. It would be distinctly out of keeping with Christian understanding of things. What Royce does is to treat God as the unifying principle of the community, the "active, indwelling purpose" which gives it its coherence. That is all right as long as we have some prior notion of the distinctiveness of God,

9. Ibid., p. 85.

something that would distinguish him from the community. The social model by itself does not provide this.

Moreover, there is the danger that in making the community the sole model of transcendence, the self will be totally absorbed into the group and thereby lost. We have had sufficient experience of mass movements in modern times to be wary of this possibility. It is important, therefore, that God not become simply a surrogate for society—even an idealized society. To insure that this does not happen, we had best consider another model to balance this one.

AGENT-IN-ACTION

One of the important insights into personal identity that has come to the fore in modern times is the recognition of just how intimately an individual's identity is bound up with that of the communities to which he belongs. The family, the nation, the social and ethnic groups to which I belong all serve to identify me as a person. Abstracted from the network of relationships in which I am situated, I am no longer the same person. In fact, I may have difficulty even thinking of myself as a person. Being a person is so much a matter of being in relationship to other persons that it is difficult to see how anyone could conceive of himself as a person except in relationship to other persons.

On the other hand, there is the persistent fear of being absorbed into the group, of losing one's identity as an individual by being treated simply as part of a larger whole. Royce's concept of loyalty seeks to avoid this danger by requiring a commitment on the part of the individual to the cause for which the community exists. In that way individuality is transcended but not abnegated. It is as a self that I have my identity in community. All too often, though, this commitment is lacking, and the individual is simply absorbed into the group. Then there is neither selfhood nor community: there is instead a single, collective identity.

What is needed, it would seem, is a model of transcendence that can bridge the gap between individual and society. An exclusively inward transcendence, such as represented by the model of elusive subjectivity, does not do this, and neither does an exclusively social transcendence. Somehow we need to preserve the integrity of the self without isolating the self from others. We need to overcome the hiatus between self and others without a complete loss of self. One way in which this might be done is through the concept of action. An action is something I myself do, yet it is also something I can do with others. I am not necessarily alone when I act. In fact, certain actions require the cooperation of others; they are simply not possible apart from corporate effort. Nevertheless they remain the responsibility of the individual. An action does not cease to be *my* action simply because it is shared with others.

Action is intersubjective in another sense as well. For it is primarily through action that we have access to the subjectivity of others. If I want to know someone's mind, I will generally observe his action. I will try to see what he is up to. Action establishes a bridge between persons. It brings them into relationship with one another and in the process also makes possible their joining together to form a community. For although a common memory and a common expectation are important to a community, it is primarily the common activity in which the members are engaged which makes them a community. Through common effort on behalf of a common good, they are enabled to transcend their individual differences.

But is it really the case that action provides access to the subjectivity of the person? Would it not be more accurate to say that we observe persons' actions and infer what they intend? After all, I do not know for certain from observing a person's action what he intends. He might have something quite different in mind from what I think he does. All that I can say for certain is that he is exhibiting a certain sort of bodily behavior. From what I observe I may surmise that he has certain objectives in view, but I cannot know. Only he can "know" what is on his mind.

This is a common picture of how we are related to one another, and it is not surprising that it should have arisen. For, in fact, we do frequently misunderstand one another's intentions and act at cross purposes with one another. Still it is a misleading picture, since it supposes that a person's history is divisible into two separate histories: an inner history of what goes on in his mind and an outer history of his bodily behavior. The inner history is known only to the person himself, whereas the outer history can be known both to the person himself and others. The inner event, in some mysterious way, causes the outer event. From observing the outer event we infer the inner event. Yet this is an impossible account, since we would never be in a position to infer the inner event unless it were already implicit in the outer event.

Imagine trying to infer from a purely physiological description of a person's behavior—the movement of the muscles, the relative position of the limbs, the repetitiveness or lack of repetitiveness in the movements—what exactly he intended. It would be impossible. He could be intending almost anything, or nothing. Unless we can somehow see what he intends *in* what he is doing, we have no basis on which to make the inference. On the other hand, if we can see an implicit intention in the person's action, we have no reason to infer a prior event that is purely inward and private. It is enough that we can see *what* the person is up to: that suffices to explain his action. And even if we cannot tell what he is doing, it will not help to posit a mysterious cause antecedent to the action. For that explains nothing. It would be better to ask the person what he is doing or wait to see how his action turns out.

No one has made the case against the "two histories" view of the person more forcefully or eloquently than Gilbert Ryle. His *Concept of Mind* is a massive assault on what he calls the official doctrine or "the dogma of the ghost in the machine." In place of what is essentially a dualistic conception of the person, he proposes a more unified view taking as his clue the action of the person. Action, he maintains, is not to be thought of as two events, one mental and the other physical, but as one event, mental-and-physical. "I try to show that, when we describe people as exercising qualities of mind, we are not referring to occult episodes of which their overt acts and utterances are the effects; we are referring to those overt acts and utterances themselves."[10] When I describe someone's action, whether it be something highly cerebral such as chess playing, or something more mundane such as mailing a letter, I am describing the workings of his mind. For these things do not "just happen." They occur because someone intends for them to. They imply the subjectivity of the person.

Consider the example of a clown feigning clumsiness. His stumblings may be visibly similar to those of a drunk, yet there is an obvious difference: his are done on purpose. The clown intends to trip in order to make us laugh. His tumbles are the work of his intelligence. Does that mean they are preceded by a mental event, such as the thought "I will make like I am stumbling"? Is this what makes his

10. Gilbert Ryle, *The Concept of Mind* (New York: Barnes & Noble, 1949), p. 25.

behavior different from that of the drunk who has no control over his actions? Not at all. For not only does the clown not have to think what he is going to do before he does it (he may, for instance, make it up as he goes along), but it makes no sense to say that it is some prior event "in the head" which makes his action purposeful. For then we should have to ask whether that prior event was itself purposeful. If it was not, it is difficult to see how it could account for the purposefulness of the action; whereas if it was, it would itself require a previous event to account for its purposefulness, and so on *ad infinitum.* The two-event theory of personal action is simply not coherent.

To act with intention is not to do two things. It is to do one thing, but to do it differently from what one would do if he were to act without intention. What sort of difference it makes to act with intention is a matter we will have to go into more fully later on, but for now it is sufficient to note that intention is implicit in action, and therefore as open to public view as action itself. If we identify subjectivity with intention, that would make subjectivity also accessible to others. It would not be something that could only be inferred from action, something that could only be known directly to the person himself. It would be within the public domain. What is more, there would be the possibility of corroboration from two distinct points of view: that of the agent and that of an observer not the agent. If we consider the ambiguity of almost any identification, but particularly identifications involving subjectivity, that is not an inconsiderable advantage.

Ryle makes a great deal out of the intersubjective character of action, even to the point of saying that "the sorts of things that I can find out about myself are the sorts of things that I can find out about other people, *and the methods of finding them out are much the same.*"[11] The fact that I have greater exposure to myself than I do to most other people means that there is more data available for making a judgment, but this is a difference only in degree. Besides, even with the additional data I have in respect to myself, I am not necessarily the best judge of myself. The difference, such as it is, is not always in favor of self-knowledge. When it comes to knowing the person as a subject, others may do a better job of it than the person himself.

That is Ryle's contention, and in a sense he is right. Others are often

11. Ibid., p. 155. Italics added.

a much better judge of a person's character and conduct than the person himself; they may even know better what a person's action means than he himself does. This is owing in large part to a greater objectivity and the tendency of persons to conceal from themselves their true intentions. But to say that the methods for finding out about oneself are the same as those for others or that the difference is only one of degree is surely to overstate the case. First-person statements of intention and feeling may not be indubitable, but they are at least distinctive. They have a different standing in the community of discourse, a different logic if you will, from second- or third-person statements. Thus, it is a matter of considerable significance whether a statement of intent is referred to an observer (however well placed) or to the agent himself. It puts the statement in an altogether different light. Likewise, deception perpetrated on another is not the same as self-deception. Without prejudicing the issue in favor of one or the other, we find a difference, a fundamental asymmetry, between "I" statements and "he" statements.

Strawson's distinction between self-ascription and other-ascription is helpful at this point. What he says about "personal predicates" applies especially to statements having to do with intention and action. For it is surely the case that I do not have to observe myself in order to say what I am doing, whereas I must observe others if I am to know what they are up to. The fact that there are these two distinct ways of ascribing predicates of action—to others on the basis of observation, to oneself apart from observation—might lead one to suspect equivocation in the use of terms. Intention ascribed to oneself means one thing; intention ascribed to another means something else. Yet, as we have seen, this is not an acceptable explanation, for it would make it impossible for anyone to teach the word *intention* (or words having to do with intention) to anyone else. It would be better to say that it belongs to the logic of terms like intention and action that they should be used unequivocally in these two distinct ways. As the agent of an action, I am in a unique position to say what I am doing. I can do so simply on the basis of intending one thing rather than another. Others can say what I am doing only by observing my action. Their identification may or may not be in agreement with mine, but in any case it will be made on different grounds.

The concept of action, as we have delineated it, is just the sort of bridge concept we have been looking for. It bridges the gap between inner and outer (what is subjective and what is objective) and also the gap between self and others (what is mine and what is not mine). Insofar as intention defines action, the subjective component is fully in view, while the bodily character of action insures accessibility to others. If we hold the two aspects together within a single, inclusive frame, there should be no problem with skepticism. There may be misunderstanding, for we are not saying that action must be unambiguous in respect to meaning; but at least there is no intrinsic problem of intelligibility. To have a concept like personal action is to be already within an intersubjective frame of reference. It should not be necessary to show how one gets from himself to others.

Still there may be a different sort of objection brought against this way of thinking, namely, that out of a passion for clarity and intelligibility we have given up the dimension of transcendence which it was our objective to uncover. Is Ryle's model of the self possibly too behavioristic? Does it not leave out the very element of subjectivity which is so important for transcendence? This is an accusation which Herbert Marcuse, for instance, makes against Ryle. He considers his analysis of the concept of mind "one-dimensional" because it treats matters such as consciousness, self, freedom in strictly behavioral terms. It reduces subjectivity to a level with everything else and does not allow the person to transcend his world.[12]

This is a weighty objection, for though it would not be correct or fair to say that Ryle simply removes the ghost of subjectivity and leaves us with a mechanistic view of the person, it is true that he puts forth a somewhat diminished view of transcendence. He seems to think that explanation of personal action must somehow be fit to the natural science model. If it does not correspond to explanation of the type "the glass broke because a stone hit it," it must belong to the type "the glass broke when a stone hit it, because it was brittle." In explaining a person's action, we do not infer to occult causes; instead we "subsume under hypothetical and semi-hypothetical propositions"—but in any case we operate within the same basic framework as we do in explaining natural occurrences.[13]

His account of explanation in respect to personal action makes it exclusively a matter of relating a person's present behavior to past or

12. Herbert Marcuse, *One-Dimensional Man* (Boston: Beacon Press, 1964), pp. 191, 203.

13. Ryle, *Concept of Mind*, p. 50.

future behavior. Thus, if I say that someone is acting from motives of vanity, I do not imply vain thoughts or feelings as the unseen cause of his action. Instead I imply that he has in the past and is likely in the future to act in certain broadly specifiable ways under certain conditions (for example, "whenever he finds a chance of securing the admiration and envy of others, he does whatever he thinks will produce this admiration and envy"). Ryle admits there are difficulties with this account. After all, when we describe someone's action as motivated in a certain way, we do not say something simply about other actions of his—actual or possible. We characterize the action he is now performing. We say that "he did what he did in a specific frame of mind."[14] Yet that could be a matter simply of the style or mood with which it was done; it need not entail anything like the transcendence of the subject. Hence the appearance of one-dimensionality remains. The tag of "behaviorist" seems to stick.

The problem with Ryle's account of personal agency is that, in spite of frequent criticism of what he calls the "contemplative idiom" in philosophy, he seldom takes the point of view of the agent. He treats action as though it were something to be observed, rather than something to be done. He does say that in observing someone's action I am "following his thoughts," not just taking in his movements. That implies something akin to an agent's point of view toward the action, but it is still not the same as actually being the agent. For an agent does not have to observe what is going on in order to know what he is doing. He has simply to intend it. His intention determines his action.

In order to bring out the difference between the two points of view, it may be helpful to compare two related ideas: action and occurrence. An occurrence is anything that happens. It need not be anything that anyone means to happen; it is enough that it happen. In explaining an occurrence, we generally try to relate it to what went before. We explain it in terms of its antecedents. If we can also bring it under some sort of general law, so much the better. The important point is that we omit all considerations of intention. We view the event without regard to the purposes and objectives of the agent.

Action, on the other hand, is inherently personal. Properly speaking, it implies intention. Thus, while it is possible to speak of the action of acid on metal or the action of a machine (apart from the purposes of

14. Ibid., p. 140.

those who made it and operate it), this is an extended use of the term. We can see this even in our own case where there are certain movements which we would consider actions and others which we would not. If I am struck on the knee with a mallet and my leg jerks, I do not call that an action. It is an occurrence, a reaction possibly, but not an action. An action is something I am prepared to take responsibility for. It is something an agent does, as opposed to something that just happens.

It is not always possible to make this distinction. In observing the behavior of another person, we are not always clear whether he is acting with intention or not—though generally we assume that he is. There is also the possibility that he may be acting with intention but we may be viewing his action impersonally, so that we do not perceive his behavior as action. There is a built-in ambiguity when it comes to human behavior: it may be seen as action or merely as occurrence, as something intended or as something that simply happened. It is even possible to view one's own action in these two ways; yet it is only as observers that we are faced with this difficulty. From the point of view of the agent, the difference is clear-cut. What I *do* is not the same as what I *undergo*. The presence of intention makes what I do significantly different from what happens to me; and even if it is not a difference I can point to, it is one of which I am intuitively aware and one which I could not possibly give up without forfeiting my identity as an agent.

By eschewing the point of view of the agent, Ryle tends to equate action with occurrence. Since he does not want to make intention into an occult occurrence antecedent to action and accessible only to the person himself, he treats it as though it were a generalization regarding the past and future behavior of the person. A person's intention is his "disposition" to behave in a certain way. But this is not how the person himself sees it—at least not at the time of his action. From the point of view of the agent, intention is a projection into the future. It goes beyond what already is. To act with intention is to have one's identity, so to speak, ahead of him. That is a different sort of transcendence than any we have considered so far, but it is transcendence nonetheless.

Where the point of view of the agent is taken seriously—where action is not simply equated with occurrence—there should be no question of one-dimensionality. The person who acts with intention stands outside of his situation at least to the extent of envisaging an alternative to it. The meaning he gives to his action is not reducible to bodily movement, since the movements he makes in the performance of the action could mean something quite different in another context. The intention itself originates with him and is not merely the consequence of antecedent circumstance and occurrence. For various reasons, action in the intentional sense involves transcendence.

Is it the sort of transcendence that can have theological application? Can we speak of God in this way? Obviously that is not an easy question to answer. In fact, it is a question that will occupy us in one way or another for the remainder of the book. But for now suffice it to say that millions of people for many hundreds of years have spoken of God in this way. If there is any one model which has been the dominant model for God in Western tradition, it has been the model of personal agency—perhaps not in exactly the form we have been speaking of, but in a form that at least approximates to it. In the biblical literature, and indeed in a good deal of philosophical writing, God is spoken of principally as Agent, as One who acts, and by his action brings things about.

In the heyday of biblical theology we heard quite a bit about the "God who acts."[15] It was claimed that this was *the* biblical understanding of God and that any other was a distortion and a misrepresentation. That view has subsequently been criticized, but largely for reasons having to do with the circumscription of God's action to history. It has not been seriously disputed that biblical writings view God as an Agent, One whose identity is in his action. Whether in the role of Creator or Redeemer, whether in the great events of history or the ordinary occurrences of nature, the God of the Bible is consistently portrayed in action. It may be that this view is no longer intelligible; but if so that is an objection of a quite different order. It leaves untouched the contention that this has been the primary way of conceiving God within the biblical-Christian tradition.

The continuing influence of this model can be seen in the prominence given to it by two contemporary thinkers with sharply divergent views on other matters: Karl Barth and Austin Farrer. Barth's background is Calvinistic and he is known for his insistence upon a strictly Christocentric approach to all theological issues. Farrer, on the

15. See, for example, G. Ernest Wright and Reginald H. Fuller, *The Book of the Acts of God* (New York: Doubleday, 1957).

other hand, is Anglo-Catholic and an impassioned defender of "natural theology." Yet both of them maintain that the only viable way of conceiving of God is as Agent: his identity is in his action. How that action is to be identified is a matter of some dispute; but there is no going behind the action to some more ultimate identity. Whatever we know of God, we know through his action.[16]

This is still a widely held view; yet increasingly it has come under attack. It has been criticized both from within the theological circle and from outside. Critics of theology maintain that it is fundamentally incoherent, that it represents an equivocal use of terms to speak of God as Agent, while theologians have begun to ask whether some other conception of God might be preferable in order to say what we want to say. It is by no means certain that the model of personal agency will continue to be the dominant model of transcendence—though it is not clear what would replace it.

THE CHOICE OF A MODEL

The quest for an acceptable model of transcendence might seem to be a merely academic exercise. Surely this is not how religions arise or develop. Individuals do not set about to formulate a concept of transcendence and then build a religion around it. Rather the religion develops as the society develops; and if there is a dominant model of transcendence, it is simply taken for granted. It may happen, though, that assumptions once taken for granted are challenged and in that way become problematical. Then it may be necessary to examine the rationale of a particular religious system and the assumptions on which it is based.

Up till now we have been primarily concerned with sorting out different alternatives. We have approached the subject of transcendence by way of the self, thinking that if transcendence is to be found anywhere it will be found in connection with self-identity. For not only do we have a certain intuitive sense of our own transcendence, but we are dependent on something like self-transcendence if we are to be related in any meaningful way to a transcendence that is beyond us. Conceptually there must be some overlap between the way in which we speak of God and the way in which we speak of ourselves.

16. Karl Barth, *Church Dogmatics* (Edinburgh: T. & T. Clark, 1936–62), vol. II/1, pp. 257 ff. Austin Farrer, *Faith and Speculation* (New York: New York University Press, 1967), pp. 104 ff.

In the course of our inquiry several alternatives have been considered. The order in which they have been taken up clearly implies a preference. Intentional action, we have said, offers the best model for interpreting transcendent reality. This is not to exclude other models, but only to say that this one is the most promising. There are several reasons for preferring it, but one of the most important is its greater intelligibility. Given the extraordinary elusiveness of God, the deep and almost impenetrable mystery which surrounds his being, this has to be a primary consideration. If we hope to shed any light at all on this difficult subject, we would do well to bring all of the understanding we can to bear. It will not do to take as our model a concept that is in itself obscure, opaque, or otherwise inaccessible to understanding.

We might, for instance, have taken causality as our model. That is a concept which has certainly played a large part in religious thinking over the years. God has frequently been spoken of as First Cause, or in some equivalent way. Moreover, it is a model which has the distinct advantage of enabling us to relate God to the world as a whole: it is not exclusively personalistic, as some models are. Yet it suffers from a high degree of unintelligibility. For what really can we know of causation outside of ourselves? We can observe its effects; we can plot the movement of particles, for instance, and formulate general laws concerning their effects upon one another; but we cannot know what it is for one thing to "cause" another, except in our own case. As an agent, I know what it is to cause something to happen, for I have only to intend certain things and they happen. As an observer of processes going on around me, I can only assume that something like the same sort of causation is taking place—and the further away I get from the sphere of the personal, the more dubious this assumption becomes.

With good reason scientists have sought to purge explanation in the natural sciences of all personal connotations. The way they have done this is to leave out the element of purpose—or at the very least intention. It is not helpful, they have found, to suppose that falling bodies "seek" the center of the earth, much as I might seek to be near someone I love. It is enough that we can formulate general laws relating mass to movement. In the case of animal behavior, it is not so clear that considerations of purpose can be omitted, but at least we ought not to impute intention to animals. As long as they cannot say what they are up to or give reasons for their actions, we cannot suppose that they act with intention.[17] This means that whatever causality we attribute to them will be different from our own, though just how different it is hard to say.

In any case, I do not have the "inside" view of natural processes that I have with respect to my own behavior or that of my fellows. I may not always know, for instance, what another person intends; but at least I know what it is to intend something and have it happen. I have no such insight into natural processes, or the behavior of animals. So if we are looking for a model of transcendence which maximizes intelligibility, we are more likely to find it in the sphere of personal agency than in the realm of natural causality.

The same argument, of course, could be advanced on behalf of the model of elusive subjectivity. After all, there too I have immediate access to what I am talking about. It would be absurd to suppose that I am only externally related to my own subjectivity. Yet this model is almost exclusively self-referential. Moreover, it is practically devoid of content. I may ascribe all manner of attributes to myself, but the self which is the subject of these ascriptions seems to elude description. It simply is.

Elusive subjectivity as a model for God may serve to underscore the subjectivity of God—God is a Subject in his own right and not merely a manifestation of the world or some process within the world—yet as the sole model of God, or even the primary model, it is deficient. It is deficient precisely in respect to intelligibility. For the most that it permits us to say about the transcendent is what it is *not*. God is not a part of the world, not an object that can be observed. He is not even describable in the way that natural processes are. He is himself and not another. Ultimately he is ineffable.

Now certainly there is no denying the mystery of God. Yet if this is all that can be said, we are virtually reduced to silence. The model of personal agency, on the other hand, permits us to speak more positively of God. It directs us to the intention of God, which need not be thought of as something totally obscure and inaccessible to us—at least not if it is an intention he has *for us*. God's intention for man could conceivably manifest itself in the events of man's history, and in that way the subjectivity of God would be preserved along with a certain objectivity.

17. For a further development of this argument, see Charles Taylor, *The Explanation of Behavior* (New York: Humanities Press, 1964).

The chief difficulty, however, with the model of elusive subjectivity is that it does not really take us outside of ourselves. It is almost exclusively inward in its orientation. That limits what can be said, but it also affects the way in which it is said. For it means we cannot seek the support of others. Social corroboration is virtually ruled out. Now it may be that every faith comes down finally to personal decision. Yet that is not the same as to say that every statement of faith must have a purely subjective meaning. Historically religious assertions have been made within a context of shared meaning. It has been assumed that they were as meaningful to others as to the person himself. With the intention-action model, it is possible to maintain that assumption without sacrificing the personal aspect.

It is only fair to say, though, that this model too has a problem of intelligibility—particularly as applied to God. For there is no way in which we can point to God, as we might to another agent. His action is not localized and neither is he. Moreover, in order to distinguish his action from our own, we make a radical distinction between the way in which he acts and the way in which we act. Whether we can do this without undermining the very intelligibility which is the strength of this model remains to be seen. But at least we begin at the point of greatest intelligibility.

A quite different sort of reason for preferring the model of personal agency is its grounding in tradition. For a rationalist that might not seem like much of a reason, yet a theological model is not the sort of thing one chooses simply because it seems reasonable. A particular way of conceiving the transcendent comes to be preferred in large part because it is congruent with the traditions in which one has been nurtured—the stories he has heard, the songs he has sung, the concepts and images that have shaped his world view. It would be a denial of all that we have learned about "historical consciousness" over the past two hundred years not to recognize this. Our most basic presuppositions—among which would certainly be included our concept of the transcendent—are to a very great extent formed by our traditions, and we had best acknowledge that fact.

This is not to say that a particular tradition must be accepted uncritically. On the contrary, traditions are continually undergoing criticism and change, and that is as it should be. The point is simply that we ought to recognize that our thinking in this area is going to be affected by tradition and that is not necessarily a bad thing. We may without compromising our integrity self-consciously take a stance within a particular tradition. But then if we do, we ought to be certain that our basic concepts are in agreement with that tradition.

For those who take their stance within the biblical tradition, it would seem that the primary model ought to be that of personal agency. Whatever we may think of the anthropomorphism of this way of speaking, there can be little doubt but that it is basic to the biblical view of God. Whatever else God is, he is an Agent. He is an active presence in the lives of people. The classic statement of this view is to be found in the Old Testament, just before the Ten Commandments, when God identifies himself to Israel as the One "who brought you out of the land of Egypt, out of the house of bondage." But it can also be seen in the priestly account of creation, in which God is pictured as the Ultimate Agent of creation, and in the teachings of Jesus, where attention is focused upon the coming reign of God. Probably, though, it is the prophets more than any others who articulate this point of view most forcefully and consistently.

As the prophets see it, God is active everywhere—in the great events of their own time and in events yet to come. His purpose may be hidden or at variance with the expectations of people, but it is efficacious nonetheless. God is sovereign over the whole of history, and nothing happens without his intention. Lest this seem completely deterministic, the prophets are equally insistent that man is an agent and that he too must act in order to be. A man's identity is not something given; it is something he must determine for himself through his choices. God has an intention for man, but man must choose whether to go that way or not. The prophetic point of view is consistently that of the agent.

A mystical, inward detachment, such as one finds in much Eastern religion, would be quite alien to the prophets. On the other hand, what we have called the social model of transcendence is thoroughly consistent with their thinking. For it is to the community of Israel that their words are primarily addressed. The intention of God, as they see it, is directed toward the future good of the people of God. If the nation as a whole is disobedient, then everyone suffers. If God is gracious, a remnant will survive—not because as individuals they are more virtuous than the rest, but because they are chosen to be representatives of the nation as a whole and bearers of the promise of God. The corporate concept is very strong in the writings of the prophets and in the Old Testament as a whole. It would be incorrect to say, therefore, that the model of personal agency is the only model of transcendence to be found in the biblical tradition.

A case can even be made for the model of elusive subjectivity. There is, after all, frequent use of the first-person "I" for God, and one instance even in which it is treated as the ultimate designation for God. In the story of the burning bush, Moses asks God by what name he is to be called and is told simply, "I am who I am." That has the appearance at least of an appeal to sheer, irreducible subjectivity. God is the Ultimate Subject: he will not be brought down to the level of an object.

Still it is as an Agent that he is primarily identified. The model of personal agency is the dominant biblical model for God. If other models are used—not to mention a diversity of images and metaphors—they are given a subordinate role. This model gives biblical literature its characteristic tone and shape. It is, for instance, one reason why narrative figures so prominently in this literature. If God is identified by what he does, it is important to keep alive the memory of his actions. Telling the story of his dealings with the people of Israel is one way of doing that. Another way would be by making projections concerning his future action—hence the importance of prophecy. Even the strong ethical orientation of biblical religion is testimony to the importance given to action. Without renouncing this tradition altogether, we have difficulty seeing how we could avoid assigning a prominent role to personal agency.

The reasons for choosing this model, however, are not simply historical or conceptual. There is also an existential consideration, the extent to which this way of speaking is congruent with one's own sense of identity. For no matter how many plausible arguments are advanced on behalf of a certain model and no matter how well grounded it may be in tradition, it is not likely to capture the imagination or focus the religious thinking of very many people if they cannot personally identify with it. Since we are speaking in any case of a reality which transcends us, it is important that we be able to relate personally to this way of speaking—and that is most likely to occur if the model corresponds to our own sense of personal identity.

Of the models we have considered, that of personal agency comes as near as any to capturing this elusive sense of personal identity. At any rate people certainly attach a great deal of importance to what they do. Even those who criticize the activist tendency in Western culture do not as a rule discredit all forms of action. What is more, everyone recognizes the difference between doing something for oneself and having it just happen. An action I myself intend is one that I can personally identify with, whereas something that just happens need not personally involve me. This is true even if the action is initiated by someone else or carried out with the cooperation of others. An action does not have to be exclusively mine in order for me to identify personally with it, but it should be something I intend. Intention is the key to the identification of a person with his action. Where intention is lacking, identification will be weak if not absent altogether. Where it is present, identification should be strong. For it is very difficult—if not impossible—for a person to disassociate himself from his intention. Intention comes very near to being synonymous with personal identity.[18]

So long as I am intending something, no matter what, I have an implicit sense of myself as subject. It is not necessary that I think of myself as pure subject. On the other hand, as one who acts with intention I am intrinsically related to others and a part of the larger world of events. I am not isolated within some mysterious "inner space," out of all relationship to everything else, as I might be if I tried to think of myself simply as a subject. Intentional action is an important way, possibly the only real way a person has of extending his identity and relating himself to the larger world. I do not, after all, come to an understanding of things merely through observation, but rather through observation accompanied by action. Through active interference with the processes going on around me, I come to understand what sort of a world it is.

Intention and action together constitute about the most important way a person has of being in the world. This would seem to be the most promising way to go about having access to a reality transcending both self and world. There may be other ways, but surely none more basic or more meaningful than this one.

18. Compare Stuart Hampshire, *Thought and Action* (New York: Viking Press, 1960), pp. 73, 126.

3. INTENTION AND ACTION

Even its critics recognize that religion has a certain internal coherence, logic, or rationale. If it is meaningless, it is not so in the way that children's verse sometimes is or that a random assortment of words from the *Oxford English Dictionary* would be. Moreover individual religions have their own particular sort of coherence. It is not always possible to specify what it is that gives a religion such as Christianity an identity distinct from other religions such as Buddhism or Islam; yet it does seem to be distinctive and to have its own particular way of saying things. For all the variety of imagery and interpretation, ritual and belief encompassed by this phenomenon we call Christianity, it does seem to have a certain basic integrity.

No doubt we will never agree on just what it is that gives a religion its internal coherence, and perhaps there is no one thing that does. I would argue, however, that one way by which religious traditions gain their coherence is through a more or less common conception of transcendence. Certainly if there is a dominant model of transcendence, it is going to affect just about everything that is said within the tradition. It is sure to influence one's conception of himself, his view of the moral life, and his expectations in respect to salvation. But most emphatically of all, it is going to make a difference in how he conceives of God. For we have no possible way of conceiving of God except by means of some model or other.

Within the Christian tradition (at least insofar as it adheres to the biblical way of speaking) the dominant model is one of personal agency. God is spoken of in terms of what he does; history is regarded as the primary sphere of meaning; man's identity is bound up with his action. If we would get inside of this tradition and attain to some sort of conceptual understanding of it, we had best get clear about this model and its implications. To some extent we have done so already, but there is more that needs to be said about personal agency before we take on that most difficult and elusive of subjects: God.

THE AGENT'S WORLD

The key to an understanding of action is intention. Intention gives a person perspective upon his situation. It enables him to envisage alternative possibilities for himself and then to choose from among these possibilities a course of action distinctly his own. If a person acts with intention, he is not locked into a rigid system of cause and effect in which whatever he does is the inevitable result of antecedent circumstance: he is at the very least free to give meaning to his action.

A person's capacity for intention distinguishes him from his situation; it enables him to stand apart from it and act decisively upon it. In this way the person may be said to transcend his situation. We may wonder, though, if this way of speaking does not have the effect of taking the person clear out of his situation. In our earlier discussion we were at pains to distinguish intentional action from mere occurrence, and the intentional form of explanation from the sort of causal explanation to be found in the natural sciences. We said that it would be misleading to attribute intention to animals, since they lack the capacity to say what they intend; and as for occurrences in nature, it would be better not even to speak of purpose. In the world of nature, other forms of explanation are more appropriate. But then what becomes of the relation between the agent and his world? Is intentional action so discontinuous with everything else that is going on as to be absurd?

It would seem that the more we succeed in exhibiting the transcendence implicit in personal agency, the greater becomes the gap between it and everything else. As an agent, however, I know that I do not exist in a private world. In order to survive I must interact with others, and with the larger world of occurrences. This larger world includes much that is nonpersonal. In fact, my own bodily behavior is not entirely personal: it is to a great extent involuntary, mechanical, unintentional. What does this do to intention? Is there any way that we can integrate personal agency into a more comprehensive scheme of things without giving up the element of transcendence?

Eventually we want to apply what we have been saying about transcendence to God. Yet traditionally God has been thought of as implicated both in the actions of persons and the processes of nature. If we limit what we say to the category of the personal, we may lose this universality. It is imperative, therefore, that we consider how intentional action is related to other forms of action, that we place the action of persons within the context of nature.

No one in recent times has done this more effectively or with greater insight and imagination than Austin Farrer. His Gifford Lectures on *The Freedom of the Will* are important for a number of reasons, but particularly for the way in which they integrate man and nature while preserving the distinctiveness of each. According to Farrer, to act freely is to act with intention.[1] Intention is what gives action its personal character. Yet not everything that happens is personal, and we would not want it to be. For many of the things we do are dependent on other things happening simply as a matter of course. My heart beats, my lungs draw air, and my blood circulates without my intending, and that is as it should be. I would not want to intend each individual heartbeat for then I would not be able to do anything else. Similarly when I drive a car, I expect it to perform most of its operations automatically. I certainly would not want it to exhibit an intention of its own. The agent's world is of necessity both personal and nonpersonal.

What the two have in common is that they both involve interaction. I interact with persons, but I also interact with the natural environment. Consider, for instance, what it would be like to live apart from people. There would be no end to interaction. If I wanted to eat meat, I would have to seek out and kill animals, and they would be sure to offer resistance. If I were satisfied to live on a vegetarian diet, I would still have to wrest a living out of the soil; and that would involve interaction with plant life of various sorts. Then, too, there would be the elements to contend with—rain, wind, sun, and snow. It would be necessary somehow to shelter myself against their blows. No one is going to survive for long in nature or in society who does not learn how to interact effectively with various kinds of "agencies."

This is true at the elementary level; and it is true at the level of scientific technology. For no matter how much in control of things we are, we are still involved in interaction with our environment. The instruments for interaction may be quite sophisticated; the environment itself may be largely man-made; still there is the necessity to find out what is going on and adjust one's actions accordingly. The world is not simply an extension of myself. It is made up of many differ-

1. Austin Farrer, *Freedom of the Will* (New York: Charles Scribner's Sons, 1958), pp. 109 ff.

ent agencies which act upon me and affect what I do. Some exhibit intention and others do not, but they all make a difference. A person would be foolish to suppose that he could act independently of any of them.

Yet they are so diverse. Is there nothing common to the different agencies with which we interact? Farrer singles out two features which he thinks are to be found at every level of existence: pattern and force.[2] Whatever engages our agency will offer resistance of some kind. The resistance may be overpowering or it may be slight and readily amenable to our influence, but in any case there will be a force to reckon with. There should also be some sort of pattern to observe. It may not be a pattern with any discernible purpose to it. What we are calling "pattern" may be simply a matter of sheer repetitiveness; still in order for us to identify a thing as something in its own right, it must exhibit some sort of order. Our response to it will depend upon the sort of order it exhibits, together with the resistance it offers to our own agency.

The further removed we are from human agency, the more reluctant we may be to speak of the other as an agent. It is not too difficult to think of animals as agents, since their behavior is purposive, even if it is not intentional, and since we can interact with them in ways analogous to the ways in which we interact with persons. This is not so true of natural processes, such as the growth of plants or chemical reactions—though even then there is often more interaction than we acknowledge. It is sometimes supposed, for instance, that scientific method is based strictly upon observation, when a key factor is the active interference of the experimenter with the processes he is observing. If we could not disrupt natural processes, even at the subatomic level, and bend them to our purposes, we would be quite limited in our knowledge of them. Interaction is simply indispensable to our whole way of knowing. Still we may not wish to call anything we interact with an "agent."

Farrer suggests the term *activity-system* for centers of agency below the personal level (though nothing would prevent us from speaking of persons also as activity-systems). The world, as he sees it, is not itself a system but "an interaction of systems innumerable."[3] These systems

2. Ibid., pp. 178 ff.
3. Austin Farrer, *Love Almighty and Ills Unlimited* (New York: Doubleday, 1961), p. 49.

exhibit varying degrees of complexity and flexibility in their internal organization. At the lower levels, there is very little flexibility. Atomic structure and molecular structure alike are quite rigid, and rightly so, since for all that we can tell they are the base on which everything else is built. The higher up the scale of activity we go the more "self-determination" the different systems exhibit. Organisms, for instance, can do more than molecules. But persons have the greatest freedom of all. They can, in a way that no other system can, choose what they will be. They are self-determining in the full sense of the word.

That brings us back to the subject of intention. For it is intention primarily which distinguishes personal agency from other forms of agency. The ability of persons to invest their action with meaning clearly sets them apart from other activity-systems. It gives them a freedom others lack. It does not, however, take them out of the world of interacting systems altogether, and that is the point we wanted to make. Intention implies a certain transcendence in respect to the world, but not a total divorce from the world. The person who acts with intention is *in* the world but not entirely *of* it. He interacts with other activity-systems but in a way that puts him somehow "above" them.

The transcendence which goes with intention gives the person a perspective on the world and a control over it which other agents do not have. I can, for instance, bring other systems of activity under my purpose. Without their ceasing to be themselves and to function according to their own principles, they may be made to do my bidding. Rivers may be diverted from their natural channels and made to flow over man-made dams in order to provide electrical power. Yet the river itself does not change. It goes on being a river, only in the process it is made to serve human ends. In much the same way processes go on within our bodies which are strictly natural but which are made to serve personal ends. We choose what we will do with our bodies, what meaning our bodily behavior will have.

Intentional action is not destructive of action at other levels. What it does is to capture natural processes and incorporate them into a larger system of meaning. In that way they are made to bear a meaning they would not otherwise have had. If I shake hands with someone, for instance, I exercise my muscles in a way that is not unnatural but which goes beyond the merely natural in the meaning it has for both him and me. A physiologist might give a purely physical account of those muscle movements and no one would suppose they had any further meaning; yet for the agents involved they do. In fact, it is the personal meaning that is the overriding consideration. Without it the movements would not have even taken place. There would have been nothing for the physiologist to explain.

Those who would like to reduce all explanation to a single type will probably not be satisfied with this account. For it means that the same event is susceptible to more than one kind of explanation. At one level it may be explained in terms of the fairly rigid uniformity characteristic of natural processes, at another level in terms of the sort of instinctual purposiveness that animals exhibit, and at the human level in terms of intention. One sort of explanation does not exclude another, yet they are distinctive. Each has its own particular logic, and it would be a mistake to try to fit them all to the same model.

Eventually we will be speaking of yet another level of explanation, the religious or theological. Anyone who finds mixed explanation at the mundane level unacceptable is sure to object to the introduction of a further dimension of meaning, but for now our concern is simply to get clear about the form of explanation which is to serve as the model for theological explanation. If there is confusion here, there is certain to be confusion later on.

REASONS FOR ACTION

A constant source of misunderstanding is the attempt to reduce all explanation to a single type. It is supposed, for instance, that because natural occurrences are best explained in terms of antecedent circumstance and the general laws which enable us to infer from a particular set of circumstances what will occur, the action of persons must also be explained in this way. If there is such a thing as intention, it must be an event antecedent to action. Unfortunately, though, it is an unobservable event and therefore useless in making predictions. What is more, it is an event identifiable only in terms of the action it explains, so that it is questionable whether it explains anything.

Those who try to fit personal action to the natural event model invariably end up ignoring intention or treating it as something quite superfluous. Yet it is the key to explanation in the personal mode. If we would understand it, we would best set aside the natural event model and look for one more suitable. This is particularly important if we are eventually to make sense of talk about God's action. For quite clearly, if God is to be spoken of in this way, intention will be an important factor both in the identification and explanation of his action. If we do not understand this way of speaking as it applies to ourselves, we will surely be in trouble when it comes to applying it to God.

Among the various philosophers who tackled the subject of intention, one of the most successful is Elizabeth Anscombe. Her monograph entitled *Intention* provides a worthwhile point of entry into the subject. Following closely the insights of the later Wittgenstein, she argues that intention is not a private event antecedent to action, but neither is it merely a description of the action. It is a form of explanation with its own particular logic. She sets forth this logic by means of a paradigm based on the question "Why?"[4] The example she uses to illustrate her paradigm is somewhat farfetched, but the results are significant if we bear in mind that it is the logic of this particular form of explanation that she is attempting to exhibit.

The example is of a man whose action is on the face of it quite commonplace: he is pumping water. It is made more complex by the fact that the water he is pumping has been poisoned and in pumping it he is supplying water to a house whose inhabitants are plotting a war. Thus in pumping the water he is also poisoning the inhabitants of the house and possibly preventing a war. Now suppose we were to ask him, first, what he was doing, and then why he was doing it. Presumably he would say he was pumping water in order to supply the house. If we continued the questioning and he was candid with his answers, he would probably say that he was poisoning the inhabitants of the house, and beyond that that he was preventing a war. If we pressed him further, he might even say something like "I am helping to bring in the Kingdom of God" or "I am furthering the cause of world peace." It is doubtful we would want to pursue the questioning any further than that!

Two things are significant about this paradigm. One is that each successive answer to the question "Why?" reidentifies the action within a broader context. Each is more inclusive than the one before. Thus, poisoning the inhabitants includes pumping the water and getting it to them. It also includes the fact that the water is poisoned—and the man might be mistaken about that. Still he intends his action

4. G. E. M. Anscombe, *Intention* (Ithaca, N.Y.: Cornell University Press, 1958), pp. 37 ff.

as a poisoning of the inhabitants and not simply as pumping water or supplying the house; so from the point of view of the agent, it is an act of poisoning—whatever the outcome. The same may be said for the further descriptions of his action as "preventing war" and "bringing in the Kingdom of God." These, too, are ways in which he conceives of his action. They put it within an even broader context—so much so, in fact, that we may be reluctant to call them descriptions of what is going on until more of the action has transpired. Yet they do stand in continuity with the other answers in that they characterize the person's behavior by setting it within a broader context.

The other thing that is distinctive about these answers is the way in which they are ordered to one another. It is a matter of no small consequence that the man should say he is pumping water "in order to" supply the house "in order to" poison the inhabitants "in order to" prevent a war. For there are other descriptions which might have been given of the action—even descriptions he himself would accept—which would not fit within such an order. He might, for instance, have been tapping out "God save the Queen" as he pumped the water, but that would have been incidental to his main interest. It would not have fit within the series. Only those descriptions which answer the question "Why?" belong within the series and they stand to one another in a particular order, an order (as Anscombe herself observes) corresponding to Aristotle's order of ends. What was an end at one stage of the questioning becomes a means to an end at the next stage, and so on until no further justification is sought. At that point the characterization of the action is perceived as complete and the action itself as self-explanatory.

If Anscombe's analysis is correct, it should be possible to explain an event not simply by reference to antecedent occurrence and general law but by inclusion within a larger description of the action as the agent conceives it and intends it. He may not always accomplish what he intends, but that is another matter. The fact remains his intention identifies his action and provides a rationale for it. In order to distinguish the two types of explanation, it may be useful to speak of the one as giving causes for the action, the other as giving reasons. It should be understood, though, that the latter is fully as explanatory as the former. Simply because the word *cause* is not used does not mean that intention is in no sense efficacious. As everyone knows who has ever done anything, intention is no mere accompaniment to action. It is what brings certain things about; otherwise the distinction between action and occurrence would be lost. What Anscombe has given us is a device for showing the unique way in which intention explains action.

Illuminating as her analysis is, though, we may wonder just how complete it is. Are there not other ways by which action might be explained that also involve intention? Consider the case of the "unknown assailant," frequently encountered in detective stories. There is no question about what happened: a man has been shot. The only question is, who did it? Who is responsible for the crime? Of course, it would be nice to know *why* he did it, and that would no doubt involve explanation of the sort Anscombe describes, but sometimes it is enough simply to know *who* did it. That is also explanation of a sort. And since it does not fit the previous model, it probably means that some other way of analyzing personal agency is necessary in order to give a full account of it.

H. L. A. Hart, an Oxford philosopher whose specialty is jurisprudence, contends that much philosophical analysis of the concept of action has been "inadequate and confusing," in large part because sentences of the form "He did it" have been regarded as primarily descriptive when their principal function is what he calls ascriptive.[5] They ascribe responsibility for a particular action to a particular agent, much as sentences of the form "This is his" ascribe rights in property. Thus, if I say that this is your coat, I add nothing to the description of the coat. I simply identify you as the owner. In the same way, if I say that you did something (whatever it might be) I identify you as the agent. Assuming we already know what you did, we add nothing to the description of the action to say that you did it. Yet it does help to explain the action. It explains by ascription rather than description.

This view of Hart's has been criticized, and he himself has acknowledged the force of much of the criticism.[6] It has been argued, for

5. H. L. A. Hart, "The Ascription of Responsibility and Rights," *Logic and Language*, ed. Antony Flew (Oxford: Basil Blackwell, 1955). A paperback edition of *Logic and Language* was published in America by Doubleday in 1965; page references to this edition will be placed in brackets following references to the original.

6. P. T. Geach, "Ascriptivism," *The Philosophical Review*, vol. 49 (1960), pp. 221–225, and George Pitcher, "Hart on Action and Responsibility," ibid., p. 226. Compare H. L. A. Hart, *Punishment and Responsibility* (New York: Oxford University Press, 1968), preface.

instance, that the term *responsibility* has quasi-moral or legal connotations not always associated with action. If I say that someone did something, I do not necessarily imply that he will be held morally or legally accountable. It may not be that sort of action. But then again, we do use the term in an extended sense to cover anything a person does on his own accord. A more telling objection would be the argument that action-words cannot have simply an ascriptive meaning for that would weaken their causal sense, which is clearly lacking in the parallel case of ascription of rights in property.

Considerations such as these have led Hart to modify his earlier position and to repudiate what one of his critics calls "ascriptivism." This is no reason, though, to reject the notion of ascription as an important component in the concept of action. For in speaking of something as an action we are not simply describing what is going on, we are also ascribing to an agent what is happening. Ascription is fully as important as description in the explanation of personal action. What Hart has done, it would seem, is to provide us with a complementary model or paradigm for explicating the concept of action. Alongside Anscombe's paradigm of "concentric description," we need to set his paradigm of "ascriptive responsibility."

Both have to do with intention, though they approach it in different ways. The descriptive approach concentrates on what the person intends, the ascriptive approach concentrates on his intending of it. Thus, in order to ascribe responsibility for action, we must establish that the person intended to do what he did. We do not as a rule hold people responsible for actions done involuntarily or inadvertently. Now it may be, as Anscombe has pointed out, that a particular action is intentional under one description and not under another.[7] My leaning against the light switch may be the cause of the lights going out, yet I may not have actually intended to turn out the lights. In that case, I am responsible for "leaning against the switch" but not for "turning out the lights." The action is ascribable to me as an agent under the one description but not under the other. Ascription and description are closely related; however, they are also distinct.

The distinction is rather nicely illustrated by something J. L. Austin said about "excuse" and "justification." We do not, he said, excuse an action by showing that it did not happen or that what happened was

7. Anscombe, *Intention*, p. 29.

good. Strictly speaking, we do not excuse actions. We excuse persons by showing that they did not in the full normative sense *do* the action. We deny that they intended it in the way that it happened. To excuse is "to argue that it is not quite fair or correct to say baldly, 'X did A.'" On the other hand, we justify an action by giving reasons for it, that is, by exhibiting the rationale of the action (as in the agent's responses to the question "Why?").[8] The one form of explanation, in other words, is ascriptive, while the other is descriptive.

A full account of personal agency requires both. It requires that someone be the agent of the action and that he have some reason for what he does. It is not always possible though to do justice to both aspects. Sometimes we know who is responsible, but not why he did what he did. Other times we know what the person's reasons are, but find that none of them is sufficient somehow, in which case we may be forced simply to acknowledge the freedom of the person to do what he will. Agency, like subjectivity, is not without a certain element of mystery.

LIMITS TO AGENCY

Up till now we have spoken of intention and action as essentially a unity. Intention, we have said, not only identifies action from the agent's point of view, it explains it. It tells us *what* the person is doing and *why* he is doing it. Thus, to take one of Ryle's examples, if I were to ask my neighbor what he was doing poking around in the ground with his shovel, he might at first simply reply that he was "digging." If I were to inquire further, asking, for instance, what he was really up to, he might tell me he was "hunting for larvae." If I continued to press him, he might then say, with a bit of annoyance, that he was "testing an ecological hypothesis." What was interesting about these responses is that each one is a statement of intention *and* a description of the action. Moreover, each one offers a further explanation of what the man was doing, since the answers would not have been essentially different if I had asked instead why he was doing what he was doing.

Intention explains action by identifying it from the point of view of the agent and by referring it to an agent as the cause. Sometimes the action is of a very far-reaching sort. The action of "testing an ecologi-

8. J. L. Austin, *Philosophical Papers* (New York: Oxford University Press, 1970), p. 124.

cal hypothesis," for instance, involves more than simply digging around hunting for larvae. It is the sort of action that may involve many agents and may not be complete in a lifetime. Still it is an identifiable action, and it is the intention of the agent which identifies it. Ecological hypotheses do not "just happen" to get tested. The testing of hypotheses is something persons *do*, and that doing presupposes intention.

Surely though not everything a person intends actually gets accomplished. It is a commonplace experience to intend one thing and have something quite different result. I intend to work in the garden but get distracted or the weather turns bad or I develop a sore back, and the job never gets done. Then what becomes of the unity of intention and action? Or what about the person who believes he is doing one thing, when in fact he is doing something quite different. He believes he is helping his friend out but he is only making matters worse for him. Does that not constitute a split between intention and action?

No analysis of intentional action would be complete which dealt only with successful actions, actions in which intention was fully embodied in action, and failed to consider aborted actions, frustrated attempts at action, actions at variance with intention. That is true even in talking about the model of intentional action. For the breakdown of a particular way of speaking can be fully as instructive as its proper functioning. It can tell us as much about what is essential to this way of speaking as the most carefully devised paradigm. It may even tell us more. For it may bring to light features which would otherwise go unnoticed.[9]

What do we mean then when we say that a person did not do what he intended? Do we mean that his intention was something quite separate from his action, or do we simply mean that he did not accomplish all that he set out to do? In order to preserve the unity of intention and action, it may be useful to point out that a failure of intention can also be interpreted as an incomplete action. If I do not do what I intend, my action is not all that it might have been. While if my intention is not fully realized in an action, it is not complete as an intention. Intention implies action; action implies intention. What happens when intentional action breaks down is that neither intention nor action is fully actualized.

9. Austin makes a similar point near the beginning of his article on excuses. Ibid., p. 128.

But what about the person who believes he is doing one thing when he is actually doing another? Is that not a clear case of intention at variance with action? Not necessarily. For as Freud has shown we often act with "unconscious intent." We act with an avowed meaning which is different from our real meaning. One reason for this is that the real meaning is unacceptable to us as agents: it does not comport with the image we have of ourselves. So effective are we at concealing our intentions both from ourselves and others that our behavior can become at times quite unintelligible without ceasing to be intentional. We should probably then speak of levels of meaning or intention. The intention at one level contradicts that at another. But we might just as well say that it was a different action at the unconscious level from what it was at the conscious level. There would still be no contradiction between intention and action. The familiar distinction between intention and action has mainly to do with the person's ability to accomplish what he intends. In other words, it has to do with the efficacy of the intention. This aspect of a person's action is frequently overlooked or obscured in the interests of not treating intention as an event separate from action; yet it is indispensable to a full understanding of personal agency. Persons are the sort of agents they are because of their ability to make things happen intentionally. There would be no point in talking about "intentional action" (as distinct from something merely happening) if intention were not in some sense "causal."

Neither Anscombe's nor Hart's paradigm bring this out with sufficient clarity. The one gives the impression that intention is simply a matter of description, the other that it has merely to do with ascription. In fact, both imply efficacy of some sort. A description is intentional if it serves to explain the action in the agent's own terms; an action is ascribable to an agent if he is in some sense the cause. The aspect of efficacy really becomes apparent, however, only when an action fails, when I do not accomplish all that I intend. Then I become aware of just how dependent I am on the efficacy of intention for anything remotely resembling personal existence. I could not even speak intelligibly were my intention not efficacious in producing the desired sounds.

Analytical philosophers, influenced by Hume, have largely overlooked the aspect of causality or efficacy implicit in intention. Because he approached causality from a strictly observational point of view he tended to reduce it to a mere sequence of occurrences without any notion of one thing making another happen. Yet if we come at it from the point of view of the agent, it is apparent that we do have it in us to make things happen, and the principal way in which we do this is by intending. I intend for my arm to move and it moves. I intend to say something and it is said. In neither case does it just happen that what I intend comes about. My intending brings it about.

If a person does not accomplish what he intends, it is generally because of outside interference. After all, I am not alone in what I do. Others also have their intentions, and they are not always in accord with mine. Besides as an agent I am often dependent on others for the accomplishment of my objectives. My action is not always mine alone. The outcome, therefore, cannot simply depend upon what I intend.

Then, too, there are internal obstacles to the full realization of an intention. Few of us are so integrated as selves that we do not fall prey to conflicting intentions, or so in possession of ourselves that we do not sometimes react involuntarily or cause things to happen inadvertently. Not everything that we do is done with full awareness of what we are doing and why we are doing it. Not only are we not always in full control of our instinctual responses, but even our intentions sometimes elude us. That may be paradoxical in view of the importance given to a person's knowing what he intends before observing what is going on, but it happens nonetheless. A person behaves in a way that he himself has difficulty understanding and only subsequently, if at all, does he come to see what it was he was doing. Then it is as though he had resumed the role of agent and were reenacting his previous action.

Fully intentional action, action in which the person accomplishes all that he intends and intends all that he does, is probably the exception rather than the rule. Certainly it is quite common for a person to fail to achieve his larger goals and objectives. The more far-reaching and inclusive an intention is the more likely that he will not be able to bring it off. It is, for instance, one thing to intend to go for a walk and quite another to intend the reconciliation of two warring factions or an end to hunger in America. Some projects are simply beyond our capability as agents, even though we may seriously intend them.

Even in such cases, however, we ought not to speak of a separation between intention and action. To the extent that the person acts in a personal way, he acts with intention. To the extent that his intention is sincere and not merely wishful thinking, it must issue in action of some kind. It would be better, therefore, to say that the person failed to accomplish all that he intended or that his action had unanticipated results. In that way we indicate the fallibility of the agent and the tensions inherent in intentional action without driving a wedge between intention and action.

Theologically it is important to recognize these tensions, since they serve indirectly to define the concept of God. Invariably those who speak of God as Agent conceive of him as One who overcomes in his own action the conflicts and limitations inherent in ours. Whether such "complete and perfect" agency is actually conceivable remains to be seen. It is, in any case, a way of indicating the transcendence of God without going outside the sphere of personal agency.

ALTERNATIVE MODELS

The model of personal agency is not a simple one. It has its own logic and rationality and certain distinct advantages over other models when it comes to indicating transcendence, but it also has its complexities and its limitations. In drawing upon the writings of several different philosophers of the analytical tradition, I have tried to give some indication of just how complex and at times elusive this way of speaking can be. It is not possible, for instance, to reduce explanation in terms of intention to a single type. Both the ascriptive and descriptive approaches are needed; yet neither one does full justice to efficacy of intention. Only at the breakdown points of personal agency do we become aware of just what kind of difference intention can make, and even then we cannot say *how* it is that intention causes something to happen. We simply know that it does.

Intention for all its intelligibility remains something of a mystery. It is a mystery precisely in respect to its ultimacy. For there is no going back of intention to some more basic form of explanation, nor any likelihood of reducing intention to something else like an antecedent event. Though there are various ways of analyzing intentional action, intention itself is irreducible. Moreover it is a "reality-principle" to which persons invariably appeal after other forms of explanation have been exhausted, as if there were no more ultimate explanation.

It is not surprising, therefore, that it should serve as a model for God. Yet is it sufficient? Can any one model suffice to identify God? After all, we are not talking simply about another person. We are not even talking about another agent in the usual sense. We are speaking of One who transcends both self and world, One who is ultimate in a way that nothing else is. Perhaps we cannot really speak of such a One; but if we can, we shall surely need more than one way of speaking. So why not more than one model?

Up till now we have gone on the assumption that it is necessary to choose from among the different models. But that need not entail choosing one to the exclusion of all others. We might prefer one and retain the others as qualifying models. A model by definition is not a literal conceptualization. So it is not inconceivable that more than one model might be used to interpret a single phenomenon. Something of the sort is already done in the empirical sciences, though it is not always acknowledged or approved of. More than one theoretical model is used to interpret the phenomenon of light, the behavior of persons, and a number of other things.[10] Reliance on a plurality of models limits what can be said with any exactness or certainty, but it also enhances our ability to be articulate about matters which go beyond strict empirical observation. Where transcendence is concerned, it would seem particularly important to have recourse to more than one model.

Every model has a certain partiality. This is good in that it provides a point of view and gives sharpness and focus to one's thinking, but it can produce distortion and misrepresentation. That is where a qualifying model can be useful. It can bring out an aspect of the subject which the primary model obscures or correct a tendency which, left unchecked, could lead to gross misunderstanding. Many of the so-called heresies which plague religious thought may very well be attributable to over-reliance on a single model. So if we are to avoid their pitfalls, we would do well to consider some alternatives to the intention-action model.

No doubt many of the models we have already considered could play this qualifying role; but there are others as well. The main thing is that we not rely upon a single point of view. If this means giving up something in the way of coherence, it is a price we must be willing to pay in the interests of maintaining the transcendence of the subject. We simply cannot expect a single model—even one with the obvious strength of this one—to permit us to say all that needs saying.

10. Ian Ramsey, *Models and Mystery* (New York: Oxford University Press, 1964), pp. 17, 40, 60. See also William H. Austin, *Waves, Particles, and Paradoxes* (Houston, Texas: Rice University Press, 1967).

Perhaps the most notable shortcoming of the intention-action model is its tendency to absorb the person into his action, so that it is difficult to speak of the person as the subject of his action. Insistence upon the intentionality of action corrects this tendency to some extent, but does not entirely eliminate it. For although intention implies a subject doing the intending, it does not identify that subject apart from what he intends. To the extent that the person intends more than one thing or has an identity which persists beyond a particular action, this approach fails us. It does not permit us to distinguish the person from his action—if only for the purpose of identifying him as the subject of his action.

Since it is generally supposed that the word *God* names an enduring Subject, and not simply an ongoing process, it may be necessary to supplement the model of personal agency with that of the elusive "I." For while this model has certain drawbacks, it also has certain advantages, notably its assertion of the persistence and irreducibility of the self. In the last analysis, it may be that all that can be said of the elusive self is simply that it is. But that is not insignificant—even from the point of view of agency. For it is indicative of a persistent subject of action and therefore irreducible source of action.

It could also counteract the tendency of the personal agency model toward determinism. For if God is thought of exclusively as Agent, and the Ultimate Agent at that, this could mean that he determines everything that happens and that there is no real freedom on the part of man. The traditional view of God is all too often equated with oppressive manipulation of persons on a cosmic scale, though that is a far remove from the biblical view of a God who seeks and creates fellowship with man. The subjective model, on the other hand, does not have this connotation. The subjectivity of one need not exclude the subjectivity of another. In fact, it could even enhance it by providing the person with an additional perspective on himself and a relationship in which he is affirmed as a self.

Leslie Dewart, in his challenging book *The Future of Belief*, takes this line in arguing against a "metaphysics of being" as the basis for Christian theism. Though he does not explicitly criticize the model of personal agency, he rejects the notion of being as an appropriate designation for God on the grounds that it does not provide for the freedom of man. It sets a limit to what man can become by his own choice. Instead of the being of God, he proposes we speak of the presence of God. The concept of presence is basically subjective. It does not imply a determinate, objective nature in the way that the concept of being does. Thus, it is possible for God to be present to man without in any way inhibiting his freedom. God's presence "reveals me to myself" in such a way that I am "more fully myself than I should be if I were not exposed to its impact."[11]

Now there is much to be said for this way of speaking, though as we have seen, it also has its limitations. One of these limitations it shares with the intention-action model: its almost exclusively personal character. As a theological model it does not shed much light upon the relationship of God to the larger world of nature. Presumably we do not speak of God being related to natural processes in a subject-to-subject way; for that would "personalize" nature beyond all recognition. But do we even want to say that everything that happens in nature is a direct enactment of God's will, as it would seem we must if we are to fall back exclusively on the model of personal agency? We are in a bind: either we deify nature or we take God out of the natural world altogether, yet neither of these alternatives is really acceptable.

The only solution is to find another model, and the most likely candidate is the much-disputed causal model. It affirms a relationship of dependence between God and the world without the implication that everything that happens in the world is the direct expression of the intention of God. Some things that happen are better thought of as occurrences than as actions. This is not to say that they do not also express the intention of God, but more indirectly than directly, and certainly not with anything like personal immediacy.

The uniformity and order implicit in natural processes could, for instance, be seen as an expression of the ordering activity of God, but it would have to be something inferred rather than observed. Likewise, it is sometimes felt that there is a "larger purpose" operative in the entire natural process—in the development from lower to higher forms of life, in the emergence of new forms of life, in the mutual adaptation of creatures to one another—but this too is a matter of inference. The traditional proofs for the existence of God come to grief precisely because it is not possible to make this sort of inference with any kind of certainty. Yet that is no reason to discard the model on which this line of reasoning is based. It may not be the best way of

11. Leslie Dewart, *The Future of Belief* (New York: Herder & Herder, 1966), pp. 176 ff.

conceiving God's relation to the world, but it does have its advantages.

Primarily it enables us to relate God to what is going on in the world without making him directly responsible for what happens. God initiates a process which is largely self-regulating, which has an integrity and a relative automony of its own, but which would not be possible without him. He creates, in other words, a world. This world is no mere extension of himself, but neither is it a machine designed to function entirely independently of his will. Not only is he responsible for the principles of order and uniformity which it exhibits, but he gives to the entire process an overall direction or meaning. "The grid of causal uniformity," as Farrer observes, "does not (to any evidence) fit so tight upon natural processes as to bar the influence of an overriding divine persuasion."[12]

The causal model also has its shortcomings, the most serious being its externality. The sort of causality we have been speaking of is not such as to provide direct or immediate access to the Agent. God may be at best inferred from the general structure of the world and the basic processes which make up the world. There is no intrinsic connection between his intention and what happens. Does this make the idea of God meaningless? Surely not, for it at least enables us to think of this as *his* world, his creation. It does not, however, have the personal meaningfulness, the "self-involving" character generally associated with religion—and it is more problematical than some other ways of speaking.

Farrer, in his *Faith and Speculation* just cited, argues that there could be some use for such a model as long as it is not taken as the primary model.[13] Personal interaction with God gives us whatever certainty we have concerning the reality of God. It also provides the basic form of our thinking about God. It must, therefore, take precedence over other models. It is quite conceivable, however, that God also acts upon us indirectly in the way that the causal model suggests. This might happen through natural processes or even through "spiritual forces" operating in the depths of our unconscious. The important thing is that we have some prior notion of what it would mean for God to act in his own right, and for this we must look to personal

12. Austin Farrer, *Faith and Speculation* (New York: New York University Press, 1967), p. 62.
13. Ibid., p. 51.

agency. For it alone provides the clue to action that is self-initiated and self-involving.

Finally, though, we need to consider whether all of these models do not fail in one important respect, namely, in dealing with the world as a totality. For if there is anything that is characteristic of religion, it is the tendency to look at the world as a whole rather than piecemeal. That is one reason why religious symbols are so elusive and not subject to the usual techniques of verification. Being inclusive in nature there is no way to test whether they are true or not. Yet the models we have been considering do not seem to have this inclusiveness. They appear limited both as to scope and reference. For quite different reasons the subjective model and the causal model place God "outside" of the world while the intention-action model fails to convey a sense of the world as a unified whole.

One way to correct for this deficiency would be to conceive of the world as God's body. That would certainly give it unity and coherence, while at the same time providing God with a sphere in which to act. But is such an idea even remotely credible? After all, my body is an organism, while the world to all appearances is not. It has no such unity as the bodily metaphor implies. What is more, we should be glad that it does not, for that would raise serious questions about the freedom and integrity of those who make up the world. It would be much better, as Farrer suggests, to think of the world as a "loose society" of agents interacting with one another. This interaction might then be thought of as forming a kind of unity, but not that of a single unitary system.

The notion of the world as a society of agents interacting with one another calls to mind the model of communal identity discussed earlier. Ideally it need not involve a loss of self, but rather an incorporation of the self into a more inclusive whole. As a member of a community I have an identity which I share with others. The scope of this "larger identity" can vary. It may extend no further than the family, but it may reach even beyond the nation. The ideal of community, as Royce observes, is in principal universal. God, as the unifying principle of the ideal community, would himself, therefore, be universal.

Probably the most significant attempt in recent times to appropriate this model and give it theological application is H. Richard Niebuhr's *Radical Monotheism and Western Culture*. Niebuhr argues in characteristic fashion that no limit can be set to the ideal of community where the "value-center" is God.[14] For God is not simply one being among others or one value among others. He is the principle of being and value, the One in relation to whom all others have being and value. Faith in him entails membership in a universal "community of being."

Niebuhr contrasts the "radical" faith which such a One elicits with the many partial or relative faiths which compete for our loyalty. The family, the social group, the nation, even mankind as a whole are limited communities with limited centers of value. They cannot possibly incorporate the whole of reality. Even nature is not inclusive enough. Only a community which has God as its Center can be truly inclusive, and the community of being is such a community.

There may be ways of indicating inclusiveness other than this way, but at least it has possibilities which ought to be explored. Particularly as long as it can be combined with other models and does not have to stand alone as the sole model for God, it has a good deal to commend it. It counteracts, for instance, some of the personalism associated with certain of the models we have considered without abandoning all contact with the self. It integrates our thinking about God into the whole of experience without imposing upon that experience a systematic unity which it does not in fact exhibit. And it expresses one of the major concerns of the biblical literature: the concern for community.

In exploring the concept of God, we would do well, therefore, to balance these different ways of speaking against one another in order that they might, if possible, qualify one another. I am certainly not proposing to abandon the model of personal agency, or even the conviction that it provides the best model of transcendence, but I am willing to acknowledge that there are alternative ways of conceiving the transcendent which might have something important to contribute. As long as we do not give up too much in the way of coherence by deploying more than one model, we ought to make as much use of them as we can. They are, after all, only models, and in the end what we seek must surely surpass anything we can express.

14. H. Richard Niebuhr, *Radical Monotheism and Western Culture* (New York: Harper & Row, 1960), pp. 31 ff.

4. THE CONCEPT OF GOD

Secularity poses the greatest challenge to religion of any of the factors in the present situation since it strikes at something quite basic to religion, its transcendent reference. Without transcendence of some sort religion becomes simply "morality tinged with sentiment" or "primitive science" or one of the other familiar residues to which it is continually reduced under the heat of skeptical criticism. Uncomfortable as we may be with certain crude understandings of transcendence, it is difficult to see how we could give up the notion of transcendence altogether and continue to think and speak religiously.

The issue then becomes one of deciding which notion of transcendence to retain. There are no doubt numerous candidates if we would look long enough and far enough; but we have chosen to remain close to home and to seek within the identity of the person the basic forms of transcendence on the assumption that if we cannot find even the suggestion of transcendence in ourselves it is doubtful we could recognize it elsewhere. This still left us with the task of deciding which of several possible conceptions of the self to take as our clue to the transcendent. In settling upon personal agency as our primary model, we recognize that it is not the only possibility, nor is it without limitations, but at least it is congruent with our religious tradition and therefore serviceable as a model for interpreting that tradition. How well it succeeds in providing us with a meaningful concept of God we now want to find out.

PROPHETIC FAITH OR MYSTICAL FAITH?

An outstanding characteristic of our time is the widespread awareness of social, historical, and cultural relativity. The pluralism within our own culture, as well as our exposure to cultures quite different from our own, has brought home to us just how relative even our most basic presuppositions are. Persons of undoubted rationality and sensibility who do not share our traditions invariably see things differently than we do. And while this relativity is apparent in all aspects of life, it is particularly apparent in the area of religion. The diversity of imagery, ritual, systems of belief, and rules of conduct is simply staggering. The great religions of the world cannot even agree on a concept of God.

The classic case is the comparison between East and West. Though there is great diversity within the religions encompassed by this broad distinction, there do seem to be fundamental differences which make it a viable distinction. Take the question of God. Hinduism and Christianity conceive of God in radically different ways. In India the notion of a Creator God seems never to have taken hold. There have been overtures in that direction, yet the prevailing view from very early times down to the present has been one of God as the pervasive Ground of Being coeternal with the world and eminently superior to it but not its actual originator. Most Buddhists do not even profess to have a concept of God. It is sufficient for them that Buddha has shown the way to put an end to suffering and attain Nirvana. But where there is a surrogate for God, such as the cosmic Buddha or the buddha-nature, the conception is clearly more Hindu than Christian.

This poses a serious problem for belief. For the concept of God is of that which is ultimate. Even if we allow that our conceptions of the ultimate are not themselves ultimate we have a problem deciding which conception is preferable or whether we should adopt any at all. A common assumption is that where there is relativity there is no basis for judgment, but this does not follow. In other areas where there is relativity we make judgments; sometimes we even make a total commitment on the basis of these judgments. The difference, of course, is that the subject matter in this case is extraordinarily elusive. God is not available for inspection; and neither are statements about God open to the kinds of verification procedures used in other areas, since verification is possible only where there are shared assumptions as to what is real. In speaking of God we are appealing to our most basic presuppositions. It is not simply an item within experience that is in question, but the total framework for interpreting experience and for deciding what is real.

My own contention would be that most of the basic differences in our various conceptions of God derive from different models of transcendence. Take the contrast between Eastern and Western religion.

With all due allowance for variations within traditions and for exceptions to the general rule, I believe that there are represented here two fundamentally different approaches to the transcendent, two basically different models. The Eastern way is essentially inward in its approach, while the Western way is primarily outward in orientation. The one relies heavily upon the model of elusive subjectivity, the other on the model of personal agency.

The inward approach to transcendence leads to what I would call a "mystical faith." It is not mystical in the sense that it is any more mysterious than any other genuinely religious faith, but only in the sense that it leads to the sort of insight and understanding traditionally associated with mysticism. For whatever else we may say about mysticism, it is inward-looking. Its techniques are designed to heighten and bring to focal awareness an otherwise implicit sense of the self as subject. Through meditation the person is encouraged to disengage himself from worldly attachments of all sorts—ranging from bodily attachment to the most subtle forms of self-attachment—and to find his identity in a pure subjectivity beyond every sort of description. The culmination of this process is the realization within oneself of an identity which transcends even the self-other distinction. There is only one reality, and the Self is that reality.

In the Eastern religions, notably Hinduism and Buddhism, this would seem to be the dominant form of transcendence. Not that all Hindus or Buddhists are mystics, but this is the prevailing form of spirituality. Even those who do not meditate tend to think of themselves in this way and to have as their goal a complete inward detachment. If you have a job to do or a duty to perform, do it with detachment. If you must act, act dispassionately and without regard for the consequences. For your "true self" is unaffected by anything you do. Your "true identity," if you but knew it, is outside the causal nexus altogether; it has no stake in this world.

This outlook is, of course, not confined to Eastern religions. It also has its spokesmen in the West. Yet it is not the dominant thought-form in Christianity and Judaism that it is in Hinduism and Buddhism. That may be because the concept of self is different. In these two biblically based religions, man is thought of primarily as an agent, as one whose identity is in his action, and who therefore is deeply implicated in the world. He transcends the world, but through interaction with it rather than withdrawal from it. His transcendence consists in the freedom with which he encounters the world and the meaning he gives to his actions in the world.

Biblical faith is not exclusively prophetic; yet the prophetic tradition is particularly expressive of this view of transcendence. In much the same way that mysticism epitomizes Eastern religion, prophecy epitomizes biblical religion. It gives it its characteristic tone and outlook. In contrast to the mystic, the prophet's basic orientation is outward rather than inward. He looks for meaning in what is going on around him and seeks to respond accordingly. He identifies with his action. Whatever future he envisions for himself, it is as an agent. He conceives of himself as part of a community, yet a community which is also active, a community with a history. The elusive self antecedent to action and unrelated to others is simply not real for him.

Neither the mystical way nor the prophetic way necessarily entails speaking of God. Yet if one is to speak of God, it will make a very great difference which of these two approaches one takes. The mystic seeks God within and is disposed to conceive of him as Pure Subject; whereas the prophet looks for God in the events of the outside world, conceiving of him as the Ultimate Agent. Either way is possible; we need to keep in mind the reasons for preferring one over the other.

Paul Tillich makes a strong case for what I have called the mystical way in an essay entitled, "The Two Types of Philosophy of Religion." He argues that there are basically two approaches to God:

> the way of overcoming estrangement and the way of meeting a stranger. In the first way man discovers *himself* when he discovers God; he discovers something that is identical with himself although it transcends him infinitely, something from which he is estranged, but from which he never has been and never can be separated. In the second way man meets a *stranger* when he meets God. The meeting is accidental. Essentially they do not belong to each other. They may become friends on a tentative and conjectural basis. But there is no certainty about the stranger man has met. He may disappear, and only *probable* statements can be made about his nature.[1]

The mystical way brings a person into an immediate relationship with God inseparable from his relationship to himself. God is not encountered as one being among others. He is not really encountered

1. Paul Tillich, *Theology of Culture* (New York: Oxford University Press, 1959), p. 10.

at all. Rather one becomes aware of him as the ultimate presupposition of thought and action. He is "known" as the self is known: reflexively. Moreover, he is known with the same immediacy and certainty as the self. We do not infer the existence of God, any more than we infer our own existence. Awareness of God is awareness of the Unconditional in ourselves.

The great advantage of this approach is that it does not lead to an alienating concept of transcendence. The "stranger-God" of which Tillich speaks in his description of the alternative to mystical religion clearly is alien to man. The relationship with God is "accidental." Statements about God are conjectural and problematical. There is nothing that can be said about God with immediacy and certainty.

Yet at least in this view God is other than man, a Subject in his own right. It is not at all clear that the God of mystical faith has an independent identity. For what is to identify him in contradistinction from ourselves if our only way of knowing him is reflexive—the way in which we know ourselves? It would seem that in conceiving of God on the model of elusive subjectivity, the mystic is left with no viable way of distinguishing God from the self. It is not too surprising then that this way tends toward pantheism and that in classical Hinduism, where it receives its most characteristic expression, the primary religious insight is the recognition that one's true identity is as Brahman or the World Soul. Brahman is certainly not the empirical self, yet neither is it other than the self. Brahman, like Tillich's Being-itself, is the dimension of ultimacy in the self and in all things. It is the ultimate "I."

This is a very different picture of God from the one in the biblical literature, where God actively engages man and where he exhibits an identity clearly distinct from man. From the vantage point of reflexive self-knowledge, it is not surprising that the biblical way of speaking of God should seem alien. But does it follow that because God is "other" he must be "alien"? Other persons, after all, are other; yet they are not necessarily alien. If they were, it would make no sense to distinguish aliens from non-aliens. Another's actions may on occasion seem strange and unintelligible, but that does not mean they are intrinsically unintelligible. In a sense, nothing is more constitutive for self-understanding than the knowledge we have of others—for all the misunderstanding that invariably accompanies it. Self-knowledge and knowledge of others are correlative, not antithetical. So in conceiving of God as other we do not necessarily conceive of him as alien—not anyway if our model for otherness is the otherness of persons.

Moreover, if we think of God as Agent, we have the added intelligibility that comes through action. Action by exhibiting intention identifies the agent in a way that we as fellow agents can comprehend. On the model of intention-in-action, God would be other than ourselves, yet accessible to us through his action. It would not be necessary to infer his intention from his action—anymore than it is necessary to infer the intention of other agents from their actions. If we have access to what he does, we have access to what he intends; and in knowing what he intends we know him. Agent identity *is* intentional identity.

Besides there are practical implications to this way of conceiving God which are lacking with the other approach. A "God who acts" is a God with whom we have actively to do. He is a God whose will we may seek, whose judgment we may accept, whose promises we may trust. In prophetic religion, man makes himself through his action; but he does not do so in isolation. He determines himself through interaction with others—and ultimately through interaction with God. How a person responds to God is decisive for who he is as a person. In the prophetic view, a God who did not act would be of no real consequence in the search for a meaningful self-identity.

So deeply rooted are we in the biblical outlook that we are disposed to take the prophetic view for granted. Although mysticism has played a part in our religious development, it has not been the primary emphasis so that when it is encountered, as in the writings of someone like Tillich, it seems like a denial of God rather than an alternative framework for conceiving of God. Yet it has a respectable history. It is an alternative worth bearing in mind. There may be something to be learned from this approach in meeting the secular challenge.

It is my conviction, however, that the reasons for preferring the model of personal agency far outweigh those on the other side. In terms of intelligibility, consistency with tradition, and agreement with some of our most basic presuppositions concerning reality, it is the more promising of the two. It is important to keep in mind, though, that the agency model is subject to the sorts of distortions Tillich speaks of. So it would be well at least to hold onto the other models as qualifiers. While taking a stance firmly within the prophetic tradition, we may nevertheless look to other traditions to correct our thinking in important ways. If our understanding of the self is complex, we should expect our understanding of God to be at least as complex.

THE PARADOX OF TWO AGENTS

In our religious tradition, God is thought of primarily as Agent, as One who acts and by his actions brings things about. Even when we are embarrassed by the anthropomorphism of this way of speaking and the appeal to miracles which usually accompanies it, we invariably fall back upon a conception of God that at least suggests that he is a "force" or a "power" to be reckoned with. Perhaps because of our pragmatic temper or because the biblical tradition is so deeply ingrained in our thinking, we are not much disposed toward a mystical conception of God.

Even when such a conception is seriously advanced it generally meets with objection. Either it is argued that this is not really a concept of God (it being assumed that God is an Agent of some sort) or that it is vacuous (lacking in empirical significance). So if we are to remain in continuity with our tradition and at the same time advance a concept of God that stands some chance of being meaningful in the present, we would do well to attend to the model of personal agency. At least it does not skirt the issues!

Can it, however, be made intelligible? Our own agency we can understand. The agency of other persons we know through observation and interaction. Even impersonal forms of activity, such as the behavior of animals, the growth of plants, or the movement of tides, are not entirely unintelligible to us since they fall within our field of observation and experimentation. But God's activity is not of this sort. It is not identifiable in the way that these other actions are. No one supposes, for instance, that it is possible to point to God. Neither can we subject his action to empirical test in the way that we do the "action" of acids, molecules, and electrons. As an Agent God is singularly elusive.

The problem is that the word *God* simply does not function as a part of our various systems of classification and explanation. The eighteenth-century scientist who was asked where God fit into his astronomical scheme and replied that he had "no need of that hypothesis" was quite correct. God's agency is not one of the factors to be considered along with mass, velocity, and relative position in calculating the movement of planets. Similarly the ethicist who insists that it adds nothing to the moral force of a particular imperative to say that God wills it need not be thought impious. For God's will is not a part of morality as such—however moral it may be to do his will. Talk of God's action, purpose, or will stands outside of these various schemes. It is not unrelated to them; yet it is not a part of them either.

The fact that we use terms borrowed from other contexts to speak of God may be the source of the confusion. We suppose that because some of the same words are used the meaning must be the same. But that would be a naïve assumption. As Wittgenstein has pointed out, words derive their meaning from their use. If they bring a certain meaning with them, it is because they have had a previous use. Thus, in applying terms like intention and action to God, we cannot be oblivious to the fact that they have other uses in other contexts. If we are not to lapse into equivocation, we must suppose that some of the meaning they have in other contexts carries over. Yet by the same token, we must not expect a theological use of terms to conform in every respect to other uses. Theology must be allowed its own logic.

The idea of different logics, or systems of meanings, is given further development by Friedrich Waismann in his concept of "language strata."[2] He argues not only that there are different systems of meaning but that they can be used to describe the same phenomena. Thus, when a scientist speaks of the chemical composition of something, he is using one language to describe it; when an interior decorator speaks of its color, texture, or durability, he is using another. Neither language is reducible to the other. We cannot from the chemist's description infer what the object would look like to an interior decorator, or from the latter's description infer the chemical composition. We might prefer one sort of description to the other. We might, for instance, consider the decorator's description vague and imprecise by comparison with the scientist's. Yet we should recognize that it is meant to serve a different purpose. By his own standards it might be quite exact. Different "languages" in this sense serve different purposes, and therefore employ different standards.

Waismann's multi-level theory of language means that for a given event different sorts of description and explanation are possible. He himself gives the example of an action, which may be viewed as a

2. Friedrich Waismann, "Verifiability," *Logic and Language*, ed. Antony Flew (Oxford: Basil Blackwell, 1955), vol. 1, pp. 128–29 [134–35]. See also "Language Strata," ibid., vol. 2., pp. 11 ff. [226 ff.].

series of movements caused by physiological stimuli or as an event having a certain meaning or purpose for the agent. The concept of action is not the same in both cases. In the one case, action is determined by causes, in the other case, by motives or reasons. If we limit the term *action* to explanations of the latter sort, we may avoid some confusion, yet we will not escape the fact that we have two ways of regarding the same event.

Moreover, the way in which we regard something can be actually constitutive of what is there for us. "Language supplies us with the means of comprehending and categorizing; and different languages categorize differently."[3] Some things simply do not appear in certain systems of thought. The language of atoms and molecules, for instance, does not permit us to talk about color and texture. The language of physiological behaviorism does not allow for assessments of motive or intention. This is not to say that language produces the fact, but rather that what we call a fact is determined in large part by the conceptual scheme we employ.

Problems arise at the point where two language strata make contact. Then there is likely to be confusion. One system of meaning may be mistaken for another; verification procedures appropriate to one may be inappropriately applied to the other; it may be supposed that we are dealing with one question when in fact we are dealing with another. To avoid confusions of this sort it is necessary to distinguish carefully between language strata, while at the same time searching out their logical connections. We need to determine as best we can what relations hold between different language strata.

If we apply this insight to the problem of God, it is quite clear that any talk of God's action must belong to a stratum different from talk of human action (or the action of natural processes, for that matter). The two simply cannot be considered on a level with one another. Though many of the same terms are used, they cannot mean the same when used of God as when used of ourselves. This also means, of course, that the two ways of speaking are not mutually exclusive. We may give an account of an event in terms of human agency (motives, purposes, desires) and still leave open the possibility of a theological account of the same event. The two accounts are not unrelated, and the major difficulties will come at just those points where they are

3. Ibid., vol. 1, p. 141 [148].

brought into relation with one another; nevertheless they are distinct, and neither one is deducible from the other. Each has its own particular logic: each answers its own particular questions.

The sorts of questions to which theology addresses itself are what Stephen Toulmin has called "limiting questions."[4] They arise at the point at which our usual methods of explanation and justification terminate. They extend the range of our reflection beyond what would be permissible on scientific, ethical, or other grounds. The sorts of answers that theology provides to these questions will not be directly contradictory or affirmative of what is said on other grounds, but they can be indirectly supportive or nonsupportive—much as belief in free will may be supportive of the type of historical explanation that appeals to the intentions of persons rather than to impersonal forces in the environment.

As for the type of question with which religion concerns itself, Toulmin gives the example of a person who at the conclusion of a lengthy moral argument asks, "Why do what is right?" If this were meant simply as an ethical question, it would show that the person had not understood the limits of moral argument. The obligation to do what is right is a presupposition of moral discourse. (Some would say it is a part of the meaning of moral terms.) It may be, however, that the person who asks this question does not mean it as an ethical question. He may mean to direct the discussion into another realm of discourse altogether: he may mean it as a *religious* question.

An example of the sort of limiting question that leads naturally to speaking of God is the question, "Why is there something and not nothing?" Within a scientific frame of reference we may explain the appearance of one thing by reference to something else. I may say that ice formed on the surface of the lake because of certain properties of water and the temperature of the air on that particular day. I may even explain the existence of the lake in terms of its geological antecedents. But to the question, "Why is there anything at all?" no such answer can be given. That sort of question takes us out of the realm of scientific inquiry altogether; it indicates the limits of scientific explanation. Some would say that it is not a real question, that it rests upon a confusion. That, however, is simply to rule in favor of scientific

4. Stephen Toulmin, *The Place of Reason in Ethics* (New York: Cambridge University Press, 1950), pp. 204 ff. Compare Ninian Smart, *The Philosophy of Religion* (New York: Random House, 1970), p. 83.

questions to the exclusion of religious questions. It remains to be seen whether it is a "real question" or not.

Persons do, after all, sometimes view the world in an attitude of wonder. They may be struck by the fact that there should be anything at all or they may be dissatisfied with explanation in terms of an endless series of causes. In either case they are looking for a different kind of explanation from what the scientist as scientist can give. The nearest analogy to the kind of explanation sought is ascription of an action to an agent. It may add nothing to the description of an action to say that someone did it; yet we can hardly say that it adds nothing to our understanding of the action. We are bound to consider an action differently if we know who is responsible. In fact, it is crucial to our viewing something as an action to know that someone is responsible. Without an agent of some sort, there can be no action in the true sense.

To ask, then, why there should be "anything at all" is, if nothing else, to see the world in its totality as action. It is to seek an ascriptive explanation of things. This sort of explanation is not to everyone's liking. Those who regard human behavior from an exclusively "behaviorist" point of view find it difficult making sense of ascriptive explanation even in respect to persons. They obviously will not be inclined to extend this form of explanation to the world as a whole. But for those whose ideal of explanation is personal, this way of thinking cannot be entirely strange and unintelligible. It is simply an extension of a form of explanation that is already familiar.

The crucial difference, of course, is the ultimacy of the ascription. Where God is the Agent, nothing is exempt; everything comes within the compass of his action. Moreover, his agency is prior to every other. It is not conditional on the action of any other agent. One way of expressing this priority would be to say that God's action is foundational to every other. Everything that is, is active in some way; his action alone is the basis of every other action. It may be impossible to conceive of such an action—that is a question we will have to attend to shortly—but at least this way of putting it enables us to place God's agency in relation to every other. He is the Agent of all agents.

To ask why there should be "something and not nothing" is one way of putting the limiting question of existence, but it is not the only way. We might also ask, "Why are things *as* they are?" Then it would not be the is-ness of things, so much as their such-ness that would be at issue. This form of the question has certain advantages over the other form. For one thing, it has to do with the determinate shape of things. The other way of putting the question is terribly abstract. The answer which it elicits is likewise abstract. We begin by inquiring about the sheer givenness of things and end by positing sheer agency without regard to purpose or intention. Presumably God acts with intention, yet intention does not figure in this form of the question except in the most general way. On the other hand, to ask why things are as they are is to make explicit the matter of intention.

Still we may be no better off when it comes to providing an answer. After all, we cannot observe the universe as a totality, as it would seem that we must if we are to ascribe a unifying purpose to it. What is more, such unity as the world has for us is strictly from our own particular vantage point; we do not have access to anything like a universal vantage point. So perhaps it is meaningless even to raise the question why things are as they are. We can explain events relative to one another, but we cannot hope to explain them relative to some ultimate purpose. It is futile even to try.

But that is only if the question depends upon our seeing things whole and complete. Actually the question can arise in a quite different way. In our dealings with the world, we discriminate things at many different levels; we consign them to different orders of activity. Thus, molecular activity belongs to one order, organic growth to another. Human behavior with all that it entails in the way of intention and action belongs to yet another order of activity. Each has its own system of organization and is fully explainable in its own terms. What these systems cannot explain, however, is the emergence of new orders. The transition from a merely molecular system of relations to an organic system is no more explainable in terms of molecular theory than the transition to intentional behavior is explainable in terms of organic theory. Maybe one feels that no explanation is required: it just happens. This would be to resort to "brute fact" for an explanation. That is a possibility, of course, but not one that most people would find satisfying. Purposive explanation, for all its inherent ambiguity, has a terminal force which other forms of explanation lack.[5]

It is not meaningless, therefore, to ask why things are as they are—even if no conclusive answer is forthcoming. It represents a desire to

5. For a further development of this argument, see Austin Farrer, *God Is Not Dead* (New York: Morehouse-Barlow, 1966), pp. 58–59.

find an intelligible basis for the world's development, to ground that development in an ultimate Cause. Yet even this may be too speculative for some. It could be argued that if we really want to speak meaningfully of God, we must show the practical relevance of this way of speaking. We must show how it relates to value considerations. If we are going to talk about God's intention, for instance, let us talk about his intention *for us*. Let us make explicit the ethical implications of what is being said. Religion and ethics may not be identical, but they are certainly closely related in the minds of most people. An analysis of religious language in terms of its ethical implications could go a long ways toward establishing its meaningfulness.

No one has pursued this line of inquiry further or with greater effect than R. B. Braithwaite in his "Empiricist's View of the Nature of Religious Belief."[6] He contends that religious assertions are primarily "declarations of adherence to a policy of action." They differ from moral assertions only to the extent that they are accompanied by "stories" which give psychological support to the intention implicit in the assertion. He takes as the epitome of the Christian religion the assertion that God is love (*agape*). In making this assertion the Christian declares "his intention to follow an agapeistic way of life." The stories he entertains (and one thinks here especially of the biblical stories, though Braithwaite himself does not cite them as examples) form the context within which the resolution to follow this way of life is made and supported. The stories need not be taken as assertions of empirical fact; it is enough that they perform this supportive function.

If Braithwaite is correct, religious assertions do not actually belong to a different level of discourse from moral assertions, though they are distinguishable from moral assertions by the stories which accompany them. But this surely will not do. The person who says that God is love is not simply declaring his adherence to a policy of love; he is expressing his conviction that there is an ultimate basis for this love. Just how realistic a conviction this is on his part is not something that can be easily or conclusively determined. In fact, it could be argued that it is more a matter of hope than of certainty. But in any case it is a basis for action, and to that extent meaningful.

6. R. B. Braithwaite, Eddington Memorial Lecture for 1955, reprinted in *Christian Ethics and Contemporary Philosophy*, ed. Ian Ramsey (New York: Macmillan, 1966).

When we ask what God intends for us, we are asking a practical question. We are asking if there is a purpose we can embrace which will not prove transitory, a good which will endure. We are asking if there is a form of life we can have confidence in, one that is ultimately secure. These are not questions which can be answered reflexively. We will not find in ourselves any such assurance, but neither will we find it in the world *per se*. Our relations with others are characterized by inconstancy and change as much as they are by faithfulness and consistency—and who is to say about the future? Only if we move outside the sphere of interpersonal relations and seek an intention grounded neither in ourselves nor our fellows can we hope to find the kind of basis for action that religion, at least in the prophetic mode, typically seeks. The weakness in Braithwaite's analysis as an analysis of religious belief lies in his refusal to credit any such transcendent reference. He denies what is at the heart of the religious way of thinking. In effect, he reduces religion to ethics.

To speak of an intention undergirding and supporting our own, an intention grounded not in ourselves or our fellows (or even some vaguely conceived "natural process"), is to move to a level of discourse different from the ethical, the psychological, or the scientific. In fact, it is to go over to a mode of discourse radically different from any other. For in speaking of God we do not speak simply of ourselves or our world as other forms of discourse do; we speak of One who transcends both self and world. To be sure, we are speaking of his action in the world and in relation to ourselves—so to that extent this way of speaking is comparable to other ways of speaking—yet the relationship is unique and the action unlike any other. The meaning, therefore, cannot be the same. It must involve quite different sorts of considerations.

For one thing, it takes us beyond the sphere of interacting agencies. Science and morality, it could be argued, are alternative ways of diagramming the interplay of agencies that make up our world. In moral discourse it may be more explicit than in scientific discourse that as one of these agencies I am in some sense distinctive. I have a capacity for transcendence that not all agents have. But that is a far remove from speaking of an Agent who transcends the whole process, whose agency originates and directs it. That is such a different way of speaking that we may wonder whether it is possible to establish *any* continuity between it and other ways of speaking.

It is certainly paradoxical. For it means, in the words of Austin Farrer, that we must speak of "two agents for an identical action."[7] This is not like saying that several agents combined to bring about a particular result. That is a familiar enough sort of explanation, but not the least bit paradoxical. It is more like saying that one agent acted through the agency of another (where agency has the connotation of office or function), but even that is misleading. For it suggests a certain incompleteness on God's part, as though he could initiate an action but lacked the capacity to carry it out. On the contrary, we should suppose that his agency is more complete than our own, surpassing in every respect what we with our limited capabilities are able to do.

A more suitable analogue is possibly to be found outside of the sphere of what we would consider "personal agency," in the supportive role which our environment plays in relation to our action. So much of what we do is, after all, dependent on our environment, that complex of interacting processes which surrounds and undergirds us. If anything in our experience can be called foundational to personal agency, it is surely the environment. Besides, though it is not personal, it is at least active. The notion of the environment as something fixed and static has long since been abandoned in the natural as well as the social sciences. The foundational elements of reality, so far as we are able to discern, are intensely active. Electrons, for instance, may not act with any purpose that we are aware of, but they are intensely active. Our own activity with its strongly purposive character is grounded in this lower level activity. We could do nothing as agents were it not for the multitude of activity-systems which support our bodily existence.

Not only that but the environment as a whole seems to exhibit a certain coherence. It makes sense to speak of "going with the grain of nature," fitting one's actions to the natural course of events. It is intelligible, therefore, to speak of the environment as supportive of what we do both in the sense of providing a basis for action and of giving direction to action. It is foundational in a way very much like what we have been saying God's agency is.

There is the danger, though, that in speaking this way we may personify the environment out of all recognition. We may come to

7. Austin Farrer, *Faith and Speculation* (New York: New York University Press, 1967), p. 104.

think of it as having an intention of its own. We do this whenever we speak of Fate. For what is Fate but the totality of environing processes and agencies conceived of as centered and purposive rather than random and disconnected? That is as true whether we locate the "center of meaning" in history as the Marxists do, or in nature as the Romantics are inclined to do. Either way we have action without an agent, and that is surely a "category mistake" of monumental proportions. If we are to speak of action at the foundational level, action of an ultimate sort, we had best be consistent and speak of an Ultimate Agent. It may be paradoxical, but at least it is not wholly without precedent or utterly incongruent with our other ways of speaking. There is an analogous way of speaking to which we can compare it.

But then how are we to conceive of this Ultimate Agent? What are we to make of an Agent we cannot observe or even point to, an Agent whose level of activity is inclusive of our own yet not identical with it, One who is unique in every respect? Is it a legitimate extension of the concept of agency even to speak in this way? It may be that we have succeeded in placing the concept of God only to discover that it is basically incoherent.

ULTIMATE AGENCY

The problem which confronts us is captured in a parable which Farrer recounts.[8] Suppose I am visiting an art gallery with a friend and as we stand before a particularly imposing picture he asks me how I would like to view it. "From close in or further back? With what daylight is available or with artificial light?" "No, thanks," I reply. "I prefer to view it as a work of Tintoretto." The incongruity of my answer shows that there has been a shift. Viewing a painting as the work of Tintoretto is a way of viewing it, but in a quite different sense from those suggested by my companion. It does not exclude these other senses, but rather takes us into a different dimension altogether.

Similarly, viewing the world as the sphere of God's action and an expression of his intention is a way of viewing it, but in a quite different sense from viewing it from the perspective of a physicist or with the categories of a sociologist. For while it does involve "seeing things in a particular light" and organizing experience in a particular

8. Ibid., p. 21.

way, it also involves a reference which neither the physicist nor the sociologist is obliged to make. It requires speaking of One who transcends both self and world, whose agency places him "outside of the picture," yet without whom the picture would not even be. Of course, there are ways, even within the religious context, to avoid referring directly to God, ways of speaking about oneself or one's world which bring a transcendent perspective to bear without making an explicit reference to the transcendent. These indirect ways of speaking about God are valid, however, only to the extent that they are backed up by a meaningful concept of God. Sooner or later we must confront the question whether it is possible to speak meaningfully of the transcendent.

By anyone's account—atheist and theist alike—God is no ordinary Agent. Tintoretto, for instance, could have been observed at his work, so that even though he is no longer living it is meaningful to speak of him as the artist responsible for a particular painting. And even if no one ever observed him, so that we had nothing to go on but the work itself, it would still be meaningful to speak of it as *someone's* work. It is, after all, the sort of thing persons do, and there are ways of distinguishing one person's work from another. None of these devices is available to us, however, when it comes to speaking of God. He is not observable; nor is it possible to distinguish events in which he was the Agent from events in which he had no part. If it is possible to identify him at all, it must be in ways quite different from the ways in which other agents are identified. The problem is whether he can be identified at all.

The most serious obstacle to be overcome is the apparent lack of anything corresponding to bodily identity. In the earlier discussion of personal identity, it was argued that bodiliness is crucial to the identification of persons as subjects. Pure subjectivity is elusive to the point of being practically inaccessible to anyone but the person himself. Even intention, which is presumably more accessible, is so only because of its embodiment in action. To be identifiable, it would seem, God must have a bodily identity. Yet that would amount to a denial of his ultimacy, for it would put his agency on a level with that of other agents.

In order to fulfill the role marked out for him by the "limiting questions" of existence, meaning, and value, God cannot be subject to the limitations of bodily agency. He cannot be restricted to a particular field of activity or a particular vantage point within the total field. He cannot be simply one agent among many, as he would be if he were a bodily agent. He cannot even be thought of as having the world for his body. For that would entail conceiving of the world as a total system, which to all appearances it is not. It would also mean that his agency would be dependent upon a buildup of activity-systems comparable to what we find in our own bodies. But that would be a denial of the priority of his agency, when the whole thrust of the limiting questions was to get back to a level of agency prior to all others. If we are to speak of God as Agent, it must be on some basis other than bodily reference.

Is this consistent with a concept of personal agency? Do we not require bodily reference in order to identify someone as the agent of a particular action? It would seem that we do; yet there is some question whether the concept actually entails it. I am, after all, able to speak of my own action without reference to my bodily behavior. I can say what I am doing without first observing my bodily movements. Even the action of other persons is not reducible to their bodily behavior. For the same movements can mean something quite different in one context from what they do in another. Moreover the same action (for instance, the action of driving a car) can encompass any number of different bodily movements. If agent identity were synonymous with bodily identity that would not be the case.

We need to be careful, though, not to go too far with this line of argument. Otherwise we shall end up with a way of speaking about God which has the character of a "private language." The great strength of the intentional action model is that it does not divorce subjectivity from observable behavior. It enables us to speak of others and their action with the same meaningfulness as our own. Agency dissociated from any sort of bodily engagement with the world is in danger of being empty and meaningless. There is the distinct possibility that we will come to think of God simply as an Intender without specific or direct connection to any action that we can observe or identify. This would seriously jeopardize, if not actually undermine, what we have set forth as our primary model of God.

Now it may be that we cannot think of God in all respects as an intentional agent, that we will need to speak of him in more than one way. The model of elusive subjectivity might then serve as a qualifying model. Undoubtedly one reason for its great appeal is that it gets around the necessity for a bodily referent—though at some sacrifice to intelligibility. The communal model is likewise less closely tied to a bodily referent than the more individualized model of personal agency. As Royce observes, the community differs from the individual in that it lacks an "internally well-knit physical organism" through which it must act.[9] Taken together these two models could serve a supplementary role in the identification of God. They are not incompatible with the intentional action model, since we do sometimes speak of action centered in a community and of a person as the subject of his actions, yet they provide a different perspective—one that is less dependent on bodily reference.

The role of a qualifying model should be to make up for limitations in the primary model. It should also help to correct for tendencies which might otherwise lead to misunderstanding. Too heavy reliance on the bodily aspect of intentional action, for instance, might lead to an idolatrous view of God. It might result in a conception of God as simply one agent among others. That would be a serious loss for the religious understanding, for it would mean that God was no longer thought of as truly transcendent. His agency would not have the ultimacy required for it to be the action of God. On the other hand, we do want to go as far as we can with the primary model. That means that in the absence of bodily identity we must look for some other way of distinguishing God's agency from others.

A partial answer to this question is already provided by the limiting questions through which we sought to place God's agency in relation to other agents. In respect to existence, purpose, and value, his agency is prior to every other. It is foundational to the total field of activity we call the world. Yet this is not enough. We also need to consider what sort of agent would be required to fulfill this role. Presumably it would be One whose agency is ultimate. But can we conceive of "ultimate agency"? Do we know what it would mean to speak of someone's action as ultimate? There is the distinct possibility that the concept of agency breaks down when applied to God—not only for lack of bodily referent, but because of the qualifications necessary to make it applicable to God.

Traditionally the way of distinguishing God's agency from every other has been by means of qualifying terms such as omnipotence,

9. Josiah Royce, *The Problem of Christianity* (Chicago: University of Chicago Press, 1968), pp. 122–23.

omnipresence, omniscience, and eternity. These terms all indicate ultimacy, yet they do so in such a way as to raise some question as to whether the concept of agency survives the qualification. Can we conceive of an agent who is all-powerful? And what would it mean to say that God is all-knowing? Substituting ultimacy for bodiliness as a way of identifying God may be no help if we cannot conceive of what ultimacy would be like in respect to agency. We need, therefore, to consider what sort of modifications the concept of agency might bear before it ceased to be meaningful.

We begin with the scope of the action. To be ultimate an action must be universal in scope: it must be all-encompassing. It cannot, in other words, be limited to a particular sphere of influence or a certain range of effects. The limiting questions by which we sought to place God's agency in relation to every other implied as much. In order to satisfy the conditions set down by these questions, God's action must encompass the whole of existence and not just one small part of it. It must be absolutely inclusive.

Can we conceive of such an action? In one sense, we obviously cannot. For none of us actually exercises that kind of influence. The scope of my action or my neighbor's action is severely limited. That is in part a consequence of being bodily agents. Our bodiliness defines to a considerable extent what we can do; it limits the scope of our action. Not that men have not devised ingenious ways of extending the range of their activities beyond their bodily limits. Technology, for instance, has greatly enhanced our potential as agents. Even bureaucratic organization, for all its shortcomings, has enlarged our capacity for action by enabling us to do things corporately that we could never do individually. Yet even with the best technology and the best organization in the world, we are limited—both as individuals and as groups. We are limited if for no other reason than because our perspective is limited. We cannot get the world as a whole into focus, and even if we could it would be from a perspective within the web of relationships which make up our world. We lack a universal point of view.

Still we are not without a certain transcendence, a certain ability to get beyond our own limited perspective. I may, for instance, enter sympathetically into the viewpoint of another—even if I cannot actually make it my own. Simply to be able to take in another's meaning is evidence that one's own perspective is not entirely limited. Then, too, there is the transcendence that comes through identification with a community and the larger purpose that generally goes with it. That is a different sort of transcendence—more inclusive in some respects, less so in others. If neither model gives us quite the inclusiveness we are after, they at least point us in the direction we want to go.

In order for God's action to be universal in scope, he must be in a position to intend for each agent from within the agent's own particular perspective and for each in relationship to the whole. The interrelatedness of agencies being what it is, that is the only way in which he can effectively act on a universal scale. If this ideal of agency is not entirely conceivable to us, it is surely not entirely inconceivable either. For it is an ideal to which we all more or less aspire. We would like to comprehend more of the world than we do, and to comprehend it in greater depth, in order thereby to act more effectively in it.

This brings us to the second mark of ultimacy, the efficacy of the action. God accomplishes all that he intends. The traditional way of expressing this has been to say that he is "omnipotent." Not that this is a particularly biblical way of speaking. It would be more in keeping with the biblical idiom to say that God is "sovereign," that his authority is beyond challenge. But simply in terms of the concept of agency, it would seem that something like omnipotence needs to be asserted. God's agency in order to be considered ultimate cannot be limited in the way that ours is. His power must be sufficient for the realization of his purposes. Whether we call this omnipotence or not will depend to a large extent on what we mean by the term *omnipotence*.

It could mean that God is the only real Agent, that whatever happens is his doing. But this would be to dissolve the paradox of two agents and to regard the world as the work of a single agent. The questions by which we sought to place the agency of God in relation to other agents were meant to avoid this outcome by establishing more than one level of agency. Besides this would ignore the distinction between action and occurrence so basic to our whole analysis. If one grants this distinction, it simply makes no sense to speak of everything that "happens" as God's "doing." God (or any other agent for that matter) only *does* what he intends. In order for an event to be considered his action it must come under his intention, and not everything that happens does.

Did we not say, though, that his action is all-encompassing, and does this not entail that he is in some sense the Agent of everything that happens? It does, but only in the sense that he is active in all things, that his intention is present in everything that happens. It does not mean that he is responsible for everything that happens under every conceivable description. He is responsible for what he intends and what he intends includes everything that happens but is not synonymous with it. We would be in a position to ascribe everything directly to God only if we were in a position to know what God intends for every particular thing, but we are not.

The point is that God's action is fully intentional. He intends all that he does and does all that he intends. That is what it means to say that he is omnipotent: his agency is complete, and therefore beyond challenge. But then what becomes of the distinction between his agency and others? Does this insistence on the efficacy of God's intention *in effect* collapse the distinction? For how can God make good on all his intentions without overriding and effectively canceling out the intentions of others? The idea of omnipotence has been a particular source of difficulty in modern times, not simply for conceptual reasons, but for practical, moral reasons. Carried to its logical conclusion, it seems to contradict the much valued autonomy of the human agent—not to mention whatever freedom and spontaneity we wish to ascribe to nature. If God is the Ultimate Agent, there would appear to be no place for any other agent.

The difficulty is in conceiving of agency at more than one level. Invariably we fall back upon conceptualizations taken from our own sphere of action and interaction. If it is the efficacy of God's action that is at issue, we suppose that it must be like our own in some way. So we "picture" God's action affecting ours in one or another of the ways ours affects others. No doubt this is inevitable, but it can be misleading, particularly if we rely upon a single picture and do not allow for the fact that it is only a picture. Efficacy, even in our own case, is difficult to conceive of; efficacy in respect to God's action is sure to be even more elusive.

One of the most common ways of approaching the subject is with a picture taken from our experience with the natural world. God, we suppose, must act upon us in a way analogous to the way in which we act upon natural agencies. Unfortunately, though, our way of affecting nature is generally to do violence to it. We disrupt its natural course of operation in order to make it serve our ends. The lumberman does violence to the forest in order to provide wood for manufacture. The carpenter does violence to the wood in order to produce a product for human consumption. This is not to say that nature itself is not violent or that men do not also contribute to the care and the replenishment of natural processes. But if our only conception of God's relation to the world is taken from our experience with nature, we will most certainly come away with the notion that he accomplishes his objectives by doing violence to ours. Talk about God "making" the world or likening his activity to that of a potter only reinforces this impression.

Another way we have of picturing God's action is taken from the political realm. We suppose that God acts upon the world in the way that a sovereign rules his kingdom. The greater the power he wields the more effective he will be at accomplishing his objectives. This has connotations of tyranny, however, when it is supposed that the power is absolute. Extending this way of thinking to God, we would suggest that he is some kind of "cosmic overlord" imposing his will by fiat upon his creatures. His intention would be the "master plan" which he has for them and which is laid on them from above. On threat of extinction they have no choice but to do what he wills. The image, in other words, is of an authoritarian system with God in the position of authority. It is softened only slightly by notions of fatherhood and kingship which suggest a benign purpose on the part of God. The relation is still essentially authoritarian and manipulative. No wonder many people consider the whole idea of divine sovereignty offensive. They would prefer a world, however chaotic and unmanageable, in which there was a free interplay of agents.

But then there is no reason to feel bound by either of these images. There are other possibilities which do not suffer from the same limitations. In fact, one of the more promising possibilities is suggested by the biblical tradition itself in the opening lines of the Genesis account of creation: "God said . . ." and it was so. If we are looking for a way of picturing God's action which indicates what sort of efficacy it has, we should at least consider the spoken word. For not only does it come as near as anything we know to being a full and complete enactment of intention, it does not have the oppressive effect on others that other forms of action have. It is not insignificant that in a supposedly free society we permit unlimited freedom of speech but not unlimited freedom of action. Speech, too, is an action of sorts, but not the sort of action that can by itself deprive another of his freedom. On the other hand, the right word from another can actually enhance a person's freedom to act. A word of forgiveness, for instance, or a word of promise can open up for a person possibilities for action that were not previously there for him.

But perhaps most significant of all, speech is uniquely self-communicative.[10] It is the primary way persons have of being present to one another. Actions, too, are communicative in this way, but speech is especially so. Thus, if you take away from a person the possibility of saying what he is up to and require that he act in silence, you will find that it is not only more difficult to discern his intention but practically impossible to get a sense of him as a person. Through what we say more than in any other way we reveal who we are. At the same time we contribute something of ourselves to the other. By making myself present to another I enrich both his subjectivity and my own.

If this is our image of how God acts, then surely there is no problem of his action inhibiting or impoverishing our own, nor any question of his agency excluding any other. Rather than supposing that he can accomplish his intention only by overpowering the creature, we ought to suppose that he does so by empowering him. That would be in keeping with the foundational character of his action and in line with the biblical conception of him as Creator. God, we are saying, acts by communicating to the creature a capacity for action of his own. In so doing he communicates something of himself—it being his nature to act.

Yet even this picture cannot stand alone; nor can it be accepted without qualification. For it leaves out the aspect of purpose crucial to any notion of intentional action. In communicating himself to the other, God invests the other with agency—in effect giving him existence as an agent. But he also bestows upon this other a determinate nature which defines what sort of agent he will be. That indicates a certain purposiveness on God's part. It does not exclude choice on the part of the creature, but it does give some direction to the choice. The creature is not free to be or do anything whatever: his action is subject to certain limitations. There is, of course, the possibility of a further intention on the part of God, one that would go beyond what is inherent in our nature, but that could simply mean a further enlargement of our action. Inasmuch as something more is intended for us, we are given a greater capacity to act.

This teleological way of speaking brings to mind the picture of the

10. Hannah Arendt, *The Human Condition* (New York: Doubleday, 1958), pp. 158–59.

agent whose successive answers to the question "Why?" had the effect of opening up an ever larger context of meaning, until finally he came to an intention impossible to realize even in a lifetime. The openness of everyone's action to this sort of meaning suggests the possibility that our actions might be included within some larger action of God. Since it would be God's action and not just ours, a successful outcome would be assured. We should still want to say that in realizing this intention God acts through, and not apart from, the creature. He does not, in other words, bypass the creature's own agency in accomplishing his objectives, but neither is he limited in what he does to what the creature has it in him by nature to do. In acting through the creature, God acts with a meaning and efficacy of his own.

That brings us to the third and final mark of ultimacy, the originality or self-determinacy with which God acts. His action is his own and not another's. It originates with himself and is expressive of himself. If it is also coincident with the action of others, it is nevertheless distinct. The distinction consists precisely in the fact that it is his, that it has no other basis than himself. God is that Agent whose action is totally his own.

The limiting questions by which we sought to place God's agency in relation to every other would seem to require such an Agent. For unless God's action is radically self-determinant, it is difficult to see how it could be foundational to the action of every other agent. There would always be the possibility of some further explanation. The questioning could go on indefinitely. Moreover, it would not be meaningful to speak of action at more than one level. For there would be no way of distinguishing God's action from the totality of the world's processes. To be distinct, God's agency must be utterly his own.

Traditionally this is what is known as the aseity of God. He is not dependent on others: he exists wholly out of himself. Whereas every other being is contingent, God is absolute. He is the sole and sufficient basis of all that he does. That cannot be said of any other agent. But then should it be said of God? The idea of aseity, like the idea of omnipotence, has been subject to considerable criticism in recent times, and not simply on conceptual grounds. It is argued that this way of conceiving God puts him completely out of touch with what is going on in the world and denies the possibility of any meaningful interaction with him. Such a conception of God is, practically, useless.

Since one of the reasons for favoring the model of personal agency is that it has practical implications, this is a serious objection. If the ultimacy of God means there is no possibility for interaction with him, then we had best go back to speaking of him simply as Subject, or in some other way that does not entail action on his part. On the other hand, we do need to distinguish God's agency from our own. It will not do to collapse the distinction between God and the world (or God and ourselves), for then there would be no point in speaking of God at all. So the question becomes whether we can maintain the uniqueness and self-determinacy of God without losing the sense of involvement with the world that goes along with action. Can God be absolute and at the same time relative?

It is interesting that Karl Barth, one of the chief modern defenders of the absoluteness of God, sees no contradiction between the two. He argues that the kind of involvement God has with the world requires radical self-determination on his part. The "absoluteness of God" means that "he has the freedom to be present with that which is not God, to communicate himself and unite himself with the other and the other with himself, in a way that utterly surpasses all that can be effected in regard to reciprocal presence, communion, and fellowship between other beings."[11] God alone is able to be "inwardly present" to another and to devote himself "wholeheartedly" to the other. That is because he alone has his being totally out of himself. He is not dependent on others for his identity.

But does this mean that God is not in any way affected by others? Barth insists that it does not. In establishing fellowship with the creature, God allows himself to be influenced. He enters into a relationship of mutuality in which what the creature does affects what he does. Still the initiative is always his. It is his intention rather than some external condition which determines what he will do. Thus, God remains the Ultimate Agent even when affected by others.

The originality or self-determinancy with which God acts assures the priority of his agency in relation to every other. If he is also responsive to the needs of the others, as we have reason to believe he is, it is on the basis of a prior commitment to their good. God's action is through and through his own. Yet for that very reason it is mysterious and elusive. Of all the marks of ultimacy we have considered this one is surely the most elusive. For there is little that can be said about sheer

11. Karl Barth, *Church Dogmatics* (Edinburgh: T. & T. Clark, 1936–62), vol. II/1, p. 313.

self-determination except that it is self-referential. It refers back to the subject of the action. Yet the subject considered in and of itself is almost impossible to comprehend.

In pursuit of an answer to the question "Why?" we are brought eventually to speak of an Agent whose intention is the sole basis of his action and whose action is therefore identical with himself, an Agent, in other words, who *is* all that he *does*. That is preferable in terms of intelligibility to an appeal to sheer brute fact, but it is scarcely distinguishable from an appeal to sheer subjectivity, which we earlier characterized as mystical. So the mystical way and the prophetic way may not be so divergent after all. Certainly they both stand in marked contrast to the sort of secularism which acknowledges nothing beyond the observable state of affairs. But in addition, they both lead ultimately to the recognition of a Subject of inexpressible depth and mystery, who in his freedom simply to be himself is the sole and sufficient ground of all that is.

MEANING AND MYSTERY

We have tried from the outset to follow the course of greatest intelligibility, yet in the end we must admit that the subject of our quest may simply elude comprehension. We do not, after all, experience "ultimate agency" in ourselves or others, so we cannot in that sense know what it means. On the basis of the limited agency we do experience, we may aspire to a more complete agency, one in which we could accomplish all that we intend, but that is mainly a hope on our part. We are in no position actually to realize such efficacy of intention. Moreover, if we could we would have no need of God, nor any way of distinguishing ourselves from God. Each person would be ultimate unto himself.

Does this mean then that the concept of God is meaningless? Not necessarily. For we ought not to expect of a concept more clarity or intelligibility than the subject allows. The Subject in this case is transcendent, and no one supposes that we can speak of the transcendent in the way that we speak of other subjects. That is implied by the denial of any ostensive reference for God. It is also implied by the use of models, metaphors, and images to speak of God. Anyone who seriously considers what he is doing when he talks about God is aware that it is different from other sorts of talk. He does not need the skeptic to point this out. In fact, more often than not he is the first to insist upon it. Just because God is transcendent, our talk about him must fail to meet the standards set by other forms of discourse. It could not be otherwise.

That leaves open the question whether the concept is actually meaningful or not. I would argue that even though God may be inconceivable, the concept of God is not meaningless. Meaning, in this instance, is not dependent on conceivability. In fact, it may be a requirement of understanding the meaning of the term *God* that one recognize the inconceivability of the subject God. The traditional theological way of putting this has been to say that God is a mystery; he exceeds our comprehension not simply in fact but in principle, so that no matter how far we go with our understanding of things we will never fully understand him. Acknowledgment of the mystery, however, ought not to be simply a way out of conceptual difficulties. We ought to be clear about what we mean by mystery, what it is about the concept of God which gives it the character of mystery, and what sort of meaning we consider to be compatible with this mystery.

The necessity of a model (or models) for speaking of God is one indication of the mystery. We have no way of speaking that refers simply and directly to God. We must borrow from other modes of discourse, which means that everything we say will carry the implicit qualification that it is not meant literally. We do this to some extent in other areas, but not to the same extent. We do not suppose that everything we say must carry this qualification. That is because in other areas we are dealing exclusively with the finite, albeit at many different levels and under many different aspects, while in theology we are dealing with the Infinite, and that takes us into a different dimension altogether.

The "dimension of ultimacy," as Langdon Gilkey calls it, is not simply one way among others of organizing experience.[12] It has more to do with the foundations of experience and with organization as such. Religious discourse, because of its foundational character, is more radical than scientific, ethical, or historical discourse. Yet by the same token it is more problematical. The presuppositional nature of theology means that we can never get God fully into focus as a subject

12. Langdon Gilkey, *Naming the Whirlwind: The Renewal of God-Language* (Indianapolis: Bobbs-Merrill, 1969), pp. 330 ff.

in his own right. He must be spoken of always in relation to something else and always with the qualification of ultimacy.

If the necessity of using a model to speak of God is one indication of the mystery, the necessity of using more than one model is a further indication. We cannot speak of God in only one way. We need to balance one model off against another. This would not be necessary if we had some independent access to the subject, but we do not. The only way that we can correct for the inevitable limitations of a particular model is by appealing to some other model. The bias of the one, it is hoped, will correct for the bias of the other. If we cannot avoid a certain relativity when it comes to speaking of God, we may at least attempt to offset it by embracing it. We may deliberately adopt more than one perspective.

These various perspectives or models do not add up to a single perspective or merge into a single model. The nearest we can hope to come to a unified view of God is to give priority to one of these models and treat the rest as qualifiers. Our dominant view of God has been and will remain that of Ultimate Agent. But that does not mean we cannot also think of him as Subject, Value Center, and Cause. After all, our own identity is not so simple and straightforward that it cannot be represented in several different ways. If it is possible—and even necessary—to adopt more than one perspective in understanding ourselves, how much more so in understanding God. The mystery we find in ourselves is as light compared to the mystery inherent in God.

For that very reason, though, no amount of analysis and clarification, and no compounding of models, is ever going to identify him exhaustively. How then can we say that the concept of God is meaningful? Certainly it is not meaningful in the way that words which name objects are meaningful, nor even in the way that words prescriptive of action are meaningful. It has a meaning distinctly its own. The way in which we have set about to exhibit that meaning is by placing the concept of God in relation to other concepts. If there is no way of identifying God other than linguistically (having ruled out ostensive identification), we ought to make the most of this particular form of identification, and one way of doing so would be to draw out the conceptual connections between speaking of God and speaking of other things.

The way in which I have tried to do this is twofold. First, by means of "limiting questions" having to do with existence, purpose, and value, I have sought to show how God's agency functions in relation to every other. Second, by means of qualifications in the concept of agency, I have tried to indicate how ultimate agency may be thought of as enhancement of personal agency.[13]

In the one case we identify God by extending the "order of explanation" beyond what is familiar and susceptible to the usual forms of verification. We press our questioning beyond the customary limits in hopes of arriving at an answer with terminal force, one that will be fully satisfying. Foundational agency of the sort attributed to God meets that condition. The other approach is to expand the concept of agency to the point where it is subject to no limits other than those inherent in the concept itself. We identify God by placing his activity on a "scale of activity" from the most rudimentary to the most exalted. If we assume that intentional action is action in the fullest sense, God by exercising complete intentionality in all that he does would be by definition the complete or perfect Agent. That in itself would distinguish him from other agents.

Both forms of identification are useful, and there is no reason to think they are not mutually complementary since both serve to identify God as Agent. Moreover they identify him as One whose agency is ultimate: God is all that he does, and God chooses to be all that he is. If agency of this sort is elusive and difficult to comprehend, it is not because it is out of all relation to everything else we know and understand but because it is without limits of the usual sort. We who are to such a considerable extent defined by our limits cannot really comprehend unlimited agency. Yet, as Farrer observes, we do seem to aspire to it. The ideal of total identification with our action and complete penetration of the world around us is implicitly sought in everything we do.[14]

So the mystery of God is not such a mystery that we cannot speak about it. What we say must be qualified and is certainly not open to the usual verification procedures, but it is not utterly unintelligible either. It has a certain coherence and consistency; but even more to the point, it is a way of speaking that we can relate to our other ways of speaking. It belongs to the larger universe of discourse in which we all participate.

13. Austin Farrer makes a similar attempt to delimit the concept of God in *Finite and Infinite* (London: Dacre Press, 1959), pp. 31–34.

14. Farrer, *Faith and Speculation,* p. 111. See also his *Freedom of the Will* (New York: Charles Scribner's Sons, 1958), pp. 109 ff.

5. GOD AND CHRIST

God is a mystery. Whatever else we say about him, we must say that. He is a mystery because he transcends us; he is not an object we can observe, classify, or manipulate; he is not an extension of ourselves or our world. To speak of God is to acknowledge a Center of Ultimacy beyond oneself and one's world.

Anything we say about such a One is sure to be problematical. It is not surprising, therefore, that many deeply religious men have been reluctant to speak of God at all. Better that we maintain a discreet and respectful silence than that we transgress upon the mystery of God by subjecting him to the vagaries and inevitable distortions of everyday discourse. It is enough that God should make his presence felt through the transformation of lives. Besides what does it matter what we *say* as long as what we *do* is in accord with the will of God? Thus a practical solution is proposed to a theoretical problem.

Unfortunately it will not work. For there is still the problem of identifying the intention of God. If we are to do the will of God, we must have some way of saying what God intends, and that involves distinguishing his agency from others. It is meaningless to talk of doing God's will if we have no way of identifying God. Up till now, however, our attempt at identification has been primarily formal. We have sought to distinguish God from other agents in terms of his status as an Agent, rather than in terms of what he intends. But we cannot leave it at that. Much of the force of this way of speaking derives from the fact that it has practical implications. If we can say nothing about what God intends, there is not much point in speaking of him as Agent.

SACRED COSMOS OR WORD OF GOD?

One of the effects of secularization has been an increasing subjectification of religion. Not only do our religious beliefs lack the support of the larger society in the sense that they are not universally shared by others; but we generally lack a context within which it is even meaningful to discuss them with others. Thus, to speak of God as Agent we should have some way of identifying his intention, some accepted procedures for determining what he is up to, but we do not. One person supposes God favors the status quo and bestows his blessing on anyone who exercises power; another thinks it is the outsider whom God loves and that he will lend his support to any revolutionary undertaking; but no one really knows and there are no accepted procedures for determining who is right. It would appear to be a purely subjective matter.

But can intention be purely subjective? Is it not built into the meaning of intention that it should be intersubjective? I may have a way of knowing my own intentions which others do not have, but this does not mean that I have no knowledge of the intentions of others, that my interpretations of their actions are simply projections. For then it would be meaningless to dispute anyone's interpretation of an action. Not only would the agent's own statement of intention be beyond challenge, but anyone else's idea of what he was up to would be incontestable since it would simply express the person's own private point of view. Yet this is not how it is with intention. We are generally able to take in one another's meaning, even when it does not agree with our own; and we are able to make judgments about the intentions of others which are not purely subjective. It even happens sometimes that another person's judgment about my intention is better than my own.

So if we extend this way of speaking to God, we should expect something like the same intersubjectivity. There need not be universal agreement as to what God intends, but there ought to be accepted procedures for saying what he is up to. It ought somehow to fall within the public domain and not be a purely private, subjective matter. Apparently, though, it is. Increasingly in modern times religion has taken on the appearance of what Wittgenstein calls a "private language." For the meaning of religious assertions, man is referred back to his own case. There are no objective criteria, no socially established norms, governing the use of religious terms. It is as though they could mean whatever a person wanted them to mean. Yet that way leads to absurdity and the breakdown of all meaning.

Granted there is a high degree of personal involvement in religious assertions. Transcendent meaning is not simply to be read off the surface of things. Still it ought not to be treated as something purely subjective and private. Otherwise it is going to cease to be meaningful to anyone—even the person himself. Meanings, after all, are learned. We must have some way of communicating them to others, some sort of objective reference, and this implies some standard other than ourselves.

If we consider what this might be in the case of God, there would appear to be two directions in which we might go. We might look for a context broad and inclusive enough to take in the full sweep of God's action, or we might hope for some definitive word from God concerning his intention. That is how it is with other agents. If we want to know what they are doing, we first try to place their action in an appropriate context. If it is a context we share with them, we generally have no difficulty making the identification. But if not, we can nearly always ask them what it is they intend. Personal testimony may not be indubitable, but it is at least a way we have of identifying the action of others. The question is whether we have anything comparable in the case of God.

Let us begin, however, with the contextual approach. When I try to understand someone else's action by placing it in the appropriate context, it is generally a quite limited context that I have in mind. If I observe my neighbor delicately removing small plants from his backyard and know him to be a botanist, I might reasonably assume that he is gathering specimens for further study elsewhere. But if I think of him primarily as a gardener, I might rather suppose that he is tending his garden. I could be mistaken in either case, but at least I have several fairly specific contexts within which to view the action. That is not how it is with God. For his action in order to be ultimate must be universal in scope. Any context which could serve to identify his action would have to be equally inclusive. Yet is such a context even conceivable?

Peter Berger, a distinguished sociologist of religion, considers it one of the primary functions of society to provide the individual with just such a context of meaning. Without it, he believes most individuals would suffer from acute anxiety. They would feel cast adrift in a "sea of meaninglessness." Society constructs this context of meaning at the same time that it forms its institutions. To a certain extent the context is a reflection of the institutional structure, yet it also has the capacity to act back upon the institutions of the society and either reinforce or change them. In any case, this larger structure of meaning is not thought of as confined to the particular institutions of a particular society but is rather regarded as inclusive of the whole of reality. "Whatever the historical variations, the tendency is for the meanings of the humanly constructed order to be projected into the universe as such."[1]

Religion, according to Berger, contributes to this tendency to give cosmological scope to what is essentially a social order of meaning by investing it with ultimate authority. Religion, in his words, "legitimates" the social order by tying it to an experience of the sacred.[2] The "cosmos," which every society requires in order to provide its members with a meaningful world view, becomes in this way a "sacred cosmos." The society's view of what constitutes the order of things is no longer (if it ever was) thought to be simply one possible system of meaning among others. Rather it comes to be seen as the ultimate state of affairs.

This absolutizing tendency is difficult to sustain in our present relativistic culture. People are less disposed than they once were to appeal to religion to legitimate their world view. Thus, the sacred cosmos has for the most part given way to a secularized cosmos. This could signal the demise of the transcendent altogether, as Berger seems to think, but it could also mean that the relation between a person's world view and his experience of the transcendent has changed. Instead of the transcendent being required in order to legitimate a particular world view, it could be the world view that comes first and provides the person with a context within which to identify the transcendent. If it is the nature of man to construct systems of meaning that are cosmic in scope, then he will do so in any case. So why should not these systems of meaning furnish the context within which it is meaningful to speak of the transcendent? They need not themselves be ultimate in order to provide access to the ultimate.

Take as an example the hierarchical world view—the "great chain of being" as it has been called.[3] No doubt at one time it was thought to be ultimate, but that may not be so important as the role it played in identifying the ultimate. In this particular world view everything is seen as related to everything else in an order of superiority and inferi-

1. Peter Berger, *The Sacred Canopy* (New York: Doubleday, 1969), p. 25.
2. Ibid., pp. 32–33.
3. Arthur O. Lovejoy, *The Great Chain of Being* (New York: Harper & Row, 1960).

ority. The higher up in the scale of being someone or something is the more worth he is assumed to possess—and that is as true of animals and angels as of men. Those higher up in the order, because of their greater worth, are invested with greater authority. Their place in the chain of command corresponds to their place in the chain of being. God, it is assumed, possesses the fullness of being in himself and therefore occupies the uppermost rung on the ladder. Pictorially he is represented as a monarch ruling his kingdom with absolute authority. But even more important for our purposes, his will is assumed to be manifest in the hierarchical order itself. Thus, in order to know what God intends, we have only to look to the natural order in which he has placed everyone and everything. Any departure from that order could only be considered a violation of his will.

This particular world view is no longer credible. It has ceased to inform not only our view of nature but our view of society as well. We might wonder, though, if some other world view has not arisen to take its place and whether it might not provide a meaningful context within which to speak of God and his will for us. Suppose, for instance, we were to transpose the hierarchical order into an evolutionary order. Then instead of looking for God's intention in the ascending order of nature, we would look for it in the forward thrust of nature and history. We would expect to see evidences of God at work in the emergence of new forms of life—new species, new social institutions, new value structures. God, we should suppose, is on the cutting edge of change, the source of the radically new wherever it manifests itself. God is the "power of the future."[4]

This way of looking at things certainly has an appeal. It not only fits in with our high regard for novelty and change but is consistent with our rather awesome sense of the future. For if there is any point in our secularized experience which could truly be said to have the character of the numinous, it is our experience of the future.[5] Scarcely anyone is indifferent toward the future; yet in our time it has assumed particular importance. Without even introducing theological considerations, we

4. Wolfhart Pannenberg, *Theology and the Kingdom of God* (Philadelphia: Westminster Press, 1969), p. 56. Others who have espoused this futuristic point of view in recent times include Carl Braaten, *The Future of God* (New York: Harper & Row, 1969), Jürgen Moltmann, *Theology of Hope* (New York: Harper & Row, 1967), and Pierre Teilhard de Chardin, *The Future of Man* (New York: Harper & Row, 1969).

5. Langdon Gilkey, "Theology in the Seventies," *Theology Today*, vol. 27, no. 3 (October 1970), p. 298.

are faced with prospects ranging all the way from total annihilation to unprecedented human fulfillment. The thought of a future so open is, to put it mildly, rather overwhelming.

So if there is, in this secular age of ours, anything like a "sacred cosmos" in Berger's sense, it is probably this future-oriented, quasi-evolutionary world view with its sense of ultimate meaning and mystery out there "ahead" of us. To speak of God within this context would presumably mean to speak of a future that is not utterly dark or ultimately threatening, a future that can be trusted to confirm rather than negate our efforts for a better life. But that is only if what God intends is good. It is not obvious that a futuristic world view by itself can provide that assurance.

Consider again how one might go about identifying the intention of God within this framework. Are we to suppose that a projection of what is to come can be made simply on the basis of what has already transpired? Can we infer God's intention from the general drift of events? Surely not, for then what would become of the novelty, spontaneity, and creativity that is supposed to characterize his action? To reduce divine agency to the level of a tendency within the general course of events is severely to depersonalize it. It is to make of his action little more than a process. In fact, if the future is only an extension of the present, it is not even transcendent; it is purely immanent.

Alternatively we might suppose that what God intends is precisely what is not a repetition of the past: the novel, the different, the unexpected. But then we have no way of anticipating the future. The only insight we have into divine intention comes after the fact. We may retrospectively decide that God has determined the emergence of some new form of life or the actualization of some new system of values, but that can tell us nothing of what is to come. What God is doing now, the future that he is preparing for us, is without precedent. It is radically new and different. Such a viewpoint toward the future certainly does not lack transcendence and mystery. It is an awesome prospect that the future might be utterly unlike anything we now know. Yet supposing it is, what can we do about it? Unlike the other approach this one seems to lack relevance. It posits a future about which we can do nothing. We can try to be open and receptive to what is to come, but that is about all. It is a viewpoint scarcely distinguishable from fatalism.

The futuristic framework by itself does not permit us to speak of God as personal. Neither does it provide a basis for identifying God's intention with any sort of particularity. The most that we can say is that the world's development, as we have been able to reconstruct it, exhibits certain general characteristics whose ultimate origin we assume to be God. But can this suffice as an identification of the action of God? According to Barth, it cannot. What is called for is a "particular event," a "definite happening within general happening." Only then can we speak of God's action as the "source, reconciliation, and goal" of all other happenings.[6] On the basis of what has been said about intention and action, we should have to agree. Without particularity of some sort, it is simply not meaningful to speak of action in the personal sense.

But if context alone cannot give particularity and immediacy to the action of God, what other recourse have we? Our only alternative would appear to be some sort of "word" on the part of God, a personal declaration of intention such as one agent might give to another. Yet what could possibly count as the "word of God"? Quite apart from the validity of specific claims to speak for God, there is some question whether it is even meaningful to talk in this way. After all, God is not a bodily agent. He is not ostensively identifiable; and neither should we suppose is he audibly identifiable. How then can we conceive of him addressing man and declaring his intention to him?

If we consider what has historically been put forth as the word of God, we are struck by the fact that it invariably takes the form of a story. Particular events are singled out for ascription to God. These events are thought to be particularly indicative of what God intends. His agency is not confined to these events, yet they are in some sense more revealing than others. The stories themselves are various. Some come very close to being strict historical narrative (one thinks especially of the Old Testament account of David's reign and certain New Testament stories of Jesus); others are more legendary (such as the Joseph story and the birth narrative); while many are simply mythological (that is to say, have no historical basis that we can ascertain). Yet they all serve in one way or another to identify the action of God. They purport, at least, to express the intention of God.

Perhaps Braithwaite was right then to single out the story as an

6. Karl Barth, *Church Dogmatics* (Edinburgh: T. & T. Clark, 1936–62), vol. II/I, p. 264.

essential element in religious discourse. But, if so, he misconstrued its function. The story is not told simply to lend "psychological support" to a policy of action—though it could have that effect. It is told in order to give particularity and intelligibility to the action of God. Without an identifying word of some sort, it would not be meaningful to speak of God active in the world. The stories fulfill this function. They say what God is up to. Apart from these stories, there would be no point in saying, as Braithwaite does, that the assertion "God is love" epitomizes the Christian religion. For that statement is no more than a summary of what is disclosed in the various stories which make up the Christian tradition. It has no independent standing either as a prescription for action or as a description of God's action in general. It is meaningful only if the stories themselves are meaningful as identifications of God's action.

But then why should it be necessary to tell a story in order to do this? Why not simply state in the form of a proposition what God intends? Probably we could, but that would not be so personally revealing as the other way. After all, the most revealing way we have of speaking about persons and their action is to tell their story.[7] To list the accomplishments of a person, or even to describe in a general way what he did in his lifetime, is not the same as to tell his story. Only by adopting a form of expression approximating the event itself do we succeed (if at all) in capturing the dynamic, personal quality of the action, and only in this way do we identify the person as the subject of the action. A person's story identifies him as a unique, unsubstitutable individual in a way that nothing else can.

So if it comes to a choice between identifying God contextually or in terms of the various stories told about him, there should be no question of the direction in which we ought to go. Not only is the latter form of identification more personal, it is also more particular. It individuates God in a way that other, more generalized forms of identification do not. Yet it may not be necessary to choose. An appropriate context, such as the one just discussed, could serve to relate stories taken from religious tradition to the present situation. In that way it could enable us to say what God is doing here and now. If we are to speak meaningfully of God as Agent, we should have both an identifying "word of God" and an identifying context, a "sacred cosmos," within which to apply that word.

7. Hannah Arendt, *The Human Condition* (New York: Doubleday, 1958), p. 167.

Still it is the word that is crucial. If nothing counts as God's word, we are in the dark as to what God intends. We have no way of actually saying what God is up to—now or in the future. In the Christian tradition, one particular story, the story of Christ and his action, is put forth as the definitive word of God. So if we are looking for a test case, this would appear to be it. If we can make no sense of the claim that Christ is God's word for us, there is little likelihood that we will find much meaning in this whole way of speaking.

THE SELF-ENACTED PARABLE

If it were not such a commonplace, it would undoubtedly seem odd that a religious tradition such as Christianity should claim for a person the status of God's word. It would not seem unusual that a person should speak about God in a way that others would consider decisive. In that case he might be said to have the "final word" on the subject of God. But to say that he himself *is* that word is something else again. This implies that he has his identity as God's word, that in speaking of him one speaks also of God. This is a claim that needs to be examined—not for its truth so much as for its meaning. For if it is not meaningful to speak in this way, the whole way of speaking about God that we have been considering is in trouble.

Let us begin by considering what sort of personal identity is to be ascribed to Christ. After all, if he is to have his identity as God's word, it will make a difference what sort of identity he has. Could we say, for instance, that it is primarily as an elusive subject that he has his identity? That is a viewpoint which has had considerable appeal in the modern period going back at least to the time of Schleiermacher. For it solves a great many problems having to do with the historical accuracy of the biblical narratives and the gap between Jesus' time and our own. A purely subjective identity is, for instance, no more accessible to objective, historical method than it is to direct, empirical observation. We are, therefore, no worse off than disciples when it comes to knowing Christ. Historical research cannot secure the identity of Jesus for the Christian, but neither can it jeopardize it.

That is in a way reassuring, but it also makes the identity in question extraordinarily elusive. It allows someone like Bultmann to accept with equanimity the most skeptical conclusions regarding "the historical Jesus," but does not permit him (or us) to say much that is concrete or particular about "the Christ of faith." He is the elusive subject, the mysterious "I," standing back of the various words and deeds attributed to him. His presence, like Ryle's "ghost in the machine," is only to be inferred from what he does. He is known, if at all, solely by reference back to oneself.

Not too surprisingly, this approach leads to a reflexive, essentially private interpretation of Christ. Since we cannot say anything determinate about him as a person we are obliged to speak of the effect he has on us as persons. If we cannot speak directly of Christ, we can at least speak of our own life in Christ. We can say what sort of difference he makes for a person's self-understanding. Now while that is certainly important, it is surely not all that can be said on the subject. For if Christ is truly to have an effect upon a person's self-understanding (not to mention his understanding of God) he must have more of an identity than this.

A better way of conceiving of him would be as a bodily subject. In that way he would be accessible to others, while at the same time distinct from them. As a bodily subject he would be assured of having his own identity. Moreover it would be an identity with particularity. For it is a person's bodiliness more than anything else which gives particularity to him as a subject. Take away the aspect of bodiliness and we have no real way of distinguishing one subject from another. Each person's subjectivity may be unique, but the uniqueness does not exhibit itself apart from bodiliness of some sort. If we intend to pursue the course of greatest intelligibility, this would seem to be the way to go about it.

It is an approach which also has a sound basis in biblical tradition. Not that the New Testament has much to say about the physical appearance of Jesus. Those artists who have over the years undertaken to paint a portrait of him have had to rely almost exclusively upon imagination. There is, however, the clear implication of bodily subjectivity. Jesus is not represented as a disembodied spirit. He is portrayed as eating and drinking with people, walking among them, touching them with his hand, looking at them with his eyes, and in the end feeling the force of their blows. Even in the resurrection stories, he appears bodily to the disciples. It is as though the New Testament community knew of no other way in which he could have had a distinct, personal identity.

Still, it is not his bodiliness as such which identifies him but his agency. Christ is who he is by virtue of what he does. His bodiliness is a condition of his agency, but it is not what identifies him. His action does that. This action ranges all the way from mundane, everyday occurrences, such as eating and drinking, to such highly personal transactions as healing, forgiving, comforting, and exhorting. In all of these actions he is fully himself. There is no suggestion that his identity might not be in these actions, that it might consist in an elusive subjectivity prior to or apart from what he does. He simply *is* what he *does.*

It might be objected, though, that this sort of identity is highly fragmentary. What becomes of the unity of the person when he has his identity in so many different activities? The answer is that all of these activities exhibit a single, unifying intention. They constitute, therefore, one action. Whether rightly or wrongly, the New Testament writers see in what Jesus does one event, not a series of unrelated events. That one event is the event of salvation, and it is this that gives Jesus his identity as the Christ.

Surely though not everyone saw this larger meaning in what Jesus did; otherwise he would have had more followers than he did. It is even arguable that his disciples did not see the full significance of what he did until after his death. So how can we say that this is what his actions actually meant? Obviously we cannot if meaning is to be thought of as something completely tangible—something observable and measurable with the instruments of the exact sciences. But this is not the sort of meaning we are talking about. Rather it is the higher order meaning of which the person himself is not always fully aware. Not only that, but it is the sort of meaning we should not expect to know until after the action is complete. The larger intention with which a person acts is never fully evident until the action is over—and sometimes not even then. More often than not, it is only the story which others tell about the person after he is gone that reveals the full meaning of his action.[8] This story, rather than any specific action, is what identifies him as a person.

In speaking of Christ as God's word, we are talking about his story, a story built up out of interaction with many persons over a period of time and culminating in his death and resurrection, a story with all of the particularity which action can give to a person's identity along with the clarity which comes from the spoken word. In this story he is

8. Ibid., p. 172.

set forth as a unique, unsubstitutable individual with an identifiable history. He is not merely the representative of some great idea or the symbol for a general truth. Even with the incursion of legendary elements into the story, he stands forth as a person in his own right, a person whose identity is unmistakably his own.[9]

But then we need to ask: how can his story identify God? If it is so much an expression of him as a person, how can it also be an expression of God? As a way into this question, we may be helped to consider something Farrer says, "If Christ is called Word or Logos, it is not meant that he is the lucid instance of general ideas, but that he is the *self-enacted human parable of Godhead*."[10] That way of putting it has several things to be said for it. In the first place, it makes contact with the tradition. Short of complete skepticism it is generally agreed that Jesus taught in parables. In fact, it is probably the single most characteristic form of expression he used. Secondly, these parables of his generally took a narrative form: they told a story. The telling of the story communicated something essential about God. But if the stories which Jesus himself told could do this, why not his own story? The parables could then serve as paradigms for the way in which Jesus' story tells about God. They could provide a bridge to speaking of him as God's word.

What is a parable? It is probably best described as a kind of "narrative image."[11] It tells a story, but with such compactness that it virtually amounts to a single image. The parables of the Good Samaritan, the Prodigal Son, the Wedding Feast all have this concentrated character even though they describe events which take place over a period of time. Similarly the story which the Gospels tell concerning Jesus spans a period of time, yet reaches such intensification of meaning at the moment of death that the image of the cross can, and for many Christians does, stand for the whole. Other episodes, such as Jesus' healing acts, his triumphal entry into Jerusalem, and his cleansing of the temple also have this concentrated, narrative character, though to a lesser extent. Each one tells the Gospel story in brief; each is a parable in its own right.

9. For a further development and defense of this idea, see Hans Frei, "Theological Reflections on the Gospel Accounts of Jesus' Death and Resurrection," *The Christian Scholar*, vol. 49, no. 4 (1966), pp. 263 ff.

10. Austin Farrer, "Revelation," *Faith and Logic*, ed. Basil Mitchell (Boston: Beacon Press, 1957), p. 98. Italics added.

11. Amos Wilder, *The Language of the Gospel* (New York: Harper & Row, 1964), p. 80.

There is yet another sense in which Jesus' action is parabolic, and that is the sense in which it points beyond itself to the ultimate agency of God. The parables have meaning at more than one level. They tell a story which has its own intrinsic interest, but they also exhibit meaning at a deeper level. The parable of the Prodigal Son, for instance, is not simply about the relations between a father and his sons; it is about God's relationship with man. The hearer is invited to put himself in the place of the wayward son, or alternatively his self-righteous elder brother, and thence to perceive in the actions of the father the intention of God. The story in that way becomes a "declaration of intention" on behalf of God. Without sacrificing any of its particularity it manages to set forth an image of compassionate fatherhood which has for countless numbers of people served as an identification of God.

In much the same way, the story of Jesus has become for Christians the master-image by which God's action is identified. This master-image functions in at least two ways: it focuses the action of God in relation to man, and it particularizes God's intention for man. It enables us both to make sense of what he is doing and to anticipate what he will do.

God is everywhere active—his action could not be ultimately efficacious if he were not—yet the larger intention with which he acts is not everywhere evident. That could be because his intention is not focused or particularized at any one point. An intention so inclusive as to embrace the entire created order is obviously going to elude our understanding unless it is focused at some point. Prior to Jesus' time, it was thought that the focus might be the history of Israel. The story of this beleaguered people built up over many generations is told as the story of God's dealings with mankind. The universal intent is not always evident; sometimes it is submerged in the particularity of the events narrated; yet it is generally there in the background. Israel has her identity as a representative people, whether she recognizes it or not.

A representative people is one way of dealing with the problem of particularity, and in some respects it is a very good way, but it has certain limitations. A community, for one thing, does not have the integrative potential that an individual has. Only by extension and with considerable qualification can we speak of agency centered in a community. The individuals of a community may share a common purpose; they may even unite in a common task; but they do not constitute a single agent. A community, for instance, does not intend anything. Neither can a community speak for itself. Someone must always speak for it, and that means its actions are always more ambiguous. It is not surprising, therefore, that we should find interwoven throughout the story of Israel an expressed longing for one who would embody in his own person, in his own particular story, the intention of God.

This is in fact what Christ means to the Christian. His action, as set forth in the Gospels, symbolizes all that God is trying to do with and for man. It draws into a single, intensive focus the whole range of his dealings with man both in nature and history. The various concepts and images used in the Old Testament to speak of God find a common reference in him. In the process they also take on new meaning. Kingship, fatherhood, justice, and love all acquire new connotations through the particularizing action of Christ. If we were to try to summarize this meaning in a single word, it would probably be the word *love* or *agape* (as it is in the Greek). Yet we should be cautious about adopting such summary formulations, lest we lose the very particularity which is the strength of this form of identification.

As the "self-enacted human parable of Godhead," Christ is the decisive, unsubstitutable expression of God's will on earth. There is no going back of his story to some more general truth about God, and no substituting another for him. Yet what identifies his action as the action of God? Leaving aside the question of verification, we should have some way of distinguishing his action from the action of other men if it is to have the significance claimed for it. Otherwise we are back with subjectivism. But what could this be? What could possibly identify an action as God's action?

CRITERIA OF ULTIMACY

Nowhere are our secular assumptions more in evidence than when it comes to speaking of the ultimacy of Christ. Not only does this claim involve a transcendent reference; it entails singling out a particular event as having significance over and above every other event. It challenges, in other words, both the assumption of one-dimensionality and the assumption of relativity. For this reason it has caused theologians of the modern period particular difficulty. We can with some confidence construct out of the biblical account a picture of Jesus that is historically plausible, one that places him within the context of his time and does not exceed the bounds of credibility. We can even recognize in him, in spite of the period dressing with which he comes to us, a certain basic humanity. But the claim that he represents God is another matter. The ultimacy of this claim gives us trouble.

Theologians of an earlier time would not have had our difficulty with this problem. For them there were clearly discernible marks of ultimacy implicit in Jesus' actions. There were his miracles, for instance. Certainly anyone who could calm the waters of a raging sea and restore sight to the blind or life to the dead must be no ordinary man. He must possess the power of God, for these actions are clearly the prerogative of God. Who but God could do such things?

Then, too, there were the Old Testament prophecies which he fulfilled. Long before Jesus appeared, the prophets of Israel anticipated his coming with descriptions of what he was to do and undergo. How could they have done so were it not that God had intended it all from the beginning? Unless we are to suppose that they made lucky guesses, we must assume that God had a plan of action which he declared beforehand to his chosen representatives. Their "prior word" on his behalf served to identify the subsequent action of Jesus as *his* action. Did God not say that this is what he would do?

Both the argument from miracle and the argument from prophecy have fallen on hard times. They no longer carry the conviction they once did. In part this is because of the widespread acceptance of relativity. We find it difficult to believe that God would act with such specificity and particularity. But also it is because this way of regarding Jesus seems to do violence to our scientific sensibility. It makes him an exception to the general laws of explanation which we accept as a matter of course in other areas of inquiry. Suppose, for instance, he did do some rather extraordinary things on the order of the acts of healing attributed to him. There is much that we do not understand, but we do not explain it by reference to God. As for the more outrageous claims made on his behalf, such as stilling the storm or raising the dead, we must assume that these are legendary embellishments resulting from the belief that he was the Christ, rather than evidence for the belief. The same goes for prophecy. It is more plausible to assume that the account of Jesus' action given in the New Testament was constructed in conformity with prophecy than to suppose that it is somehow confirmed by it. We simply do not think of God providing an advance plan of action and are suspicious of those who claim to have one.

That leaves us, however, with no real way of identifying God's action in the world. If we are to speak of certain events as uniquely his doing, we must have some way of distinguishing them from events which are not in the same sense ascribable to him. Without something like the traditional appeal to miracle and prophecy this could prove exceedingly difficult. Yet it would seem that such an appeal is out of the question. It is simply incompatible with our basic assumptions about the world.

Langdon Gilkey has brought this out with particular clarity and forcefulness in an essay entitled, "Cosmology, Ontology, and the Travail of Biblical Language."[12] He argues that it is meaningless to speak of particular events as the action of God since we no longer have an ontology which would make this way of speaking meaningful. We accept unquestioningly, he thinks, the "universal reign of causal law," and this makes the idea of special intervention on the part of God not only incredible but unintelligible. If God acts in the world, it must be by way of the natural order and in a way accessible to everyone. Thus, what was once spoken of as the particular acts of God must be reconceived as the "creative interpretations" of men. Since we do not believe that things happened any differently in biblical times than they do at present, we must assume that the biblical writers had particular insight into the meaning of the events of their time and expressed that insight in mythological form.

The "travail" of the biblical theologian arises from the fact that he tries to retain biblical categories of special divine agency without the ontology to support it. Since he no longer believes in miracles, "wondrous divine events on the surface of natural and historical life," he has no way of distinguishing special acts of God from the general activity of God. He is driven, therefore, to a subjective interpretation. What he means by the special action of God is really a special interpretation placed upon certain events by the religious community. Having given up all of the elements which (in the original account) made these events unique, he could hardly mean anything else; yet he continues to talk as though what he was saying were the same as what the biblical writers had in mind.

12. Langdon Gilkey, "Cosmology, Ontology, and the Travail of Biblical Language," *Journal of Religion*, vol. 41 (1961), pp. 194 ff.

"What we desperately need," Gilkey concludes, "is a theological ontology that will put intelligible and credible meaning into our analogical categories of divine deeds and divine self-manifestation through events." The stress here is upon the word "analogical." Having rejected the category of miracle, we are no longer able to conceive of God's action in literal or univocal terms. Yet when could we? Was it not the case that even in biblical times God's action was spoken of "analogically" (though, of course, few people had the sophistication to call it that). After all, no one ever supposed that God could be seen in the way that persons are or that his action was in every respect like the action of persons. The very concept of miracle sets God's action apart from the action of other agents. It would seem, therefore, that what is really needed is an ontology which will enable us to speak meaningfully of *particular* actions of God. That in turn may require that we reconsider the category of miracle. For without some such rubric, it is questionable how we could ever speak of a particular event as uniquely God's doing.

The common view of miracle is that it is an inexplicable event, an event which contravenes natural law and which must therefore be ascribed to a mysterious, unseen cause: God. Yet this is to miss the essential point of a miracle story. As Ramsey has pointed out, "Miracle stories are stories of characteristically personal activity, with 'God' substituted for a person-word."[13] The personal character of the event is crucial to its identification as a miracle. In terms of our earlier discussion of "language strata," that places it in a category of meaning different from what it would be regarded as a natural occurrence. There is no reason, in principle, why it could not also be explained in terms of causal antecedents and general laws, though in actual practice an event would not be identified as a miracle if it were not in some sense out of the ordinary. Everyday occurrences simply do not get singled out for that sort of attention. It is necessary, therefore, that we speak also of the exceptional character of the event even if it means an acknowledgment that customary forms of explanation fail us.

In terms of the language of personal agency, a miracle is an event that is both singularly expressive of the intention of God (which gives

13. Ian Ramsey, *Religious Language: An Empirical Placing of Theological Phrases* (New York: Macmillan, 1963), p. 169.

it its personal character) and distinctive in relation to other events (which makes it unique). It is the distinctiveness, of course, which gives us the most difficulty; yet this distinctiveness is crucial to the identification of an action of God. Without it, one action would be just like another. We would have no reason to single out a particular action and ascribe ultimacy to it. Returning to our test case, we need to consider what are the marks of ultimacy which distinguish Jesus' action from the action of other men. At the same time, we need to keep in mind whether they are such as to undermine his credibility as an agent. For if the only way of indicating ultimacy is to deny real agency on the part of the person, then the framework of two agents for a single action breaks down and the test case fails.

Let us begin with those actions of Jesus which are most commonly spoken of as miracles. What gives them their miraculous character? Is it not the remarkable scope and efficacy which they exhibit? He does things which exceed the normal range of a person's bodily power. His acts of healing and his feat of quieting the storm, for instance, give exceptional scope and efficacy to his concern for others. He is not limited in such situations to words of encouragement and exhortations to courage as most people would be. He can actually alter the situation. His power seemingly transcends the bounds of nature.

Yet it is not only nature that comes under the influence of his intention, but history as well. In our preoccupation with the view of miracle as a violation of "natural law," we have tended to overlook the miraculous character of Jesus' involvement with others. Without violating the freedom of others, he is able in his dealings with them to accomplish what he intends. He fits every action to the occasion, yet every action somehow exhibits the same basic intention. In fact, he acts with such constancy and efficacy of purpose that even those events which seem thrust upon him by circumstance or external agency can be seen to exhibit his intention.

This is particularly evident in the passion narrative. On the one hand, Jesus is portrayed as passively acquiescent to the relentless movement of events leading to his death. He is betrayed and forcibly led off to a secret trial, a public sentence, and a humiliating execution. He does not resist; he does not even speak on his own behalf. He is, to all appearances, helpless before his fate. Yet these same events are the culmination of his work, the fulfillment of his role as Messiah. They can, therefore, also be seen as his doing. In the Gesthemane episode it is made explicit that he accepted responsibility for what happened to him on that fateful night: he acted with intention.

The manner in which Jesus' detractors are made to witness on his behalf is also significant. At the trial he does not have to speak for himself; his enemies speak for him. Thus, enraged at his silence in the face of damaging testimony against him, the high priest, Caiaphas, taunts Jesus saying, "I adjure you by the living God, tell us if you are the Christ, the Son of God." To which he replies, "You have said so." Roman soldiers crown him in jest, while his executioner, Pontius Pilate, has inscribed above his cross the words "King of the Jews." So complete is his agency that he is able to enact his identity as much by what he suffers at the hands of others as by what he does on his own initiative.

What we have in mind, then, when we speak of the miraculous character of Jesus' action is really the perfection of his agency. There is no gap between what he intends and what he does, no separation between who he is and what he undergoes. He is fully effective in what he intends, fully himself in what he does. He is the complete agent. This is true even of the resurrection, that most mysterious and ultimate of events. For while there is no question but that it is God's doing, Jesus' agency having terminated with his death, it is nevertheless an authentic expression of the person of Jesus. The one who appears to the disciples is none other than the one who lived and worked among them. He is even identified in much the same way as before. Thus, in one story it is the "marks of his crucifixion," the event in which his identity was once and for all established, which identify him, in another it is the "act of breaking bread," a characteristic gesture symbolizing fellowship with others. Even in death, it seems, his action continues: he lives on.

The resurrection, of course, is the ultimate miracle. By comparison with it all others pale into insignificance. For not only is there the implication of agency that is beyond challenge, agency that does all that it intends; there is the implication of originality on the part of the agent that we can scarcely begin to comprehend. With good reason the redemption associated with Christ has been likened to a "new creation." For there is scarcely anything with which to compare his resurrection other than the creation itself. There are, to be sure, intimations of originality in the actions which precede his death—notably the action of forgiveness, which constitutes a kind of new beginning for the person—yet nothing quite like this. For that reason it is also the least conceivable of the actions which go to make up his story. Whether it is utterly inconceivable is a moot point. It is, in any case, not inconsistent with the ideal of agency which has been with us throughout this discussion.

But then what about prophecy? Does that also figure in the identification of Jesus' action as God's action in a way that we might find intelligible? The ordinary view of prophecy is that it is simply a matter of prediction. The prophet predicts something will occur and in due course it happens. Yet as Ramsey observes, there is no *religious* significance in that.[14] So even if we could establish, independently of the biblical witness to Jesus as the Christ, that he did what the prophets predicted he would do and suffered what they said he would have to suffer, that would not in itself identify his action as God's action. The significance of prophecy must lie elsewhere.

We may be helped to see the true significance of prophecy if we do not limit it to a few predictive utterances, such as are to be found in the writings of men such as Isaiah, Jeremiah, and Ezekiel, but include the whole narrative history of Israel as it was built up over many hundreds of years of oral and written tradition. This history, which includes much that is legendary and mythological, constitutes a single, inclusive story of salvation. God is the primary agent in that story, but he is not the sole agent. For it is also the story of a people, a people in search of salvation. It has its beginning in the "promise to Abraham" that he should be the father of a great nation, inheritor of a land, and a source of blessing to the families of the earth. It climaxes with the Exodus event, the deliverance of a slave people from the condition of bondage into one of relative freedom and justice. It continues with an account of their struggles both with themselves and their neighbors leading finally to a second captivity and eventual deliverance. Through it all, there is manifest the purpose of God to redeem this people, and to make of them a "light to the nations."

This work of redemption is not complete even with the return of Israel to the "promised land"—so the story goes on. Each fulfillment of a previous promise is the occasion for a new promise. Salvation, it seems, is always in the future, the purpose of God yet to be realized.

14. Ibid., p. 134.

But that is because the purpose is universal in its implications. Salvation is not limited to a particular time or place. It may be concentrated in the history of a particular people, but it is meant for all people. Thus, when the prophets, who are the chief spokesmen for this point of view and the principal interpreters of the story, speak of the coming "reign of God," they have in mind a condition of universal peace and brotherhood, one in which all men will share in the blessing of God. They even envisage the redemption of nature, such is their conception of the inclusiveness of God's purpose.

What makes prophecy so important for the identification of Jesus' action is that it provides a context within which it is possible to see what he does as part of the larger action of God. His story is seen by his followers as being continuous with the previous "story of salvation." This association is made quite explicit in the Gospel of Luke, where Jesus begins his public ministry by quoting from the prophet Isaiah to the effect that where the Spirit of the Lord is there will be "preaching of good news to the poor" and "recovering of sight to the blind." These are, of course, the sorts of things he himself does. By placing them within the context of prophecy they take on added meaning. His acts of healing, his words of encouragement to the poor, his vindication of the rejected are all seen as having redemptive significance because of being set within this context. But that means they are seen as the action of God, for in the biblical story God alone redeems.

The principal way in which Jesus relates his action to the redemptive action of God is through his proclamation of the Kingdom of God. The symbol of the Kingdom epitomized for Israel the ultimate in what God intended. It meant the full realization of his purpose for them as a people. Assuming the role of the prophet, Jesus both announced that the Kingdom was at hand and did the sorts of things associated with the Kingdom. In that way he gave credence to his word and meaning to his action. He identified what he was doing as the action of God.

His proclamation of the Kingdom also served to give universal significance to what he did. For though it is a symbol closely associated with the experiences and expectations of Israel, it has, as we have noted, wider implications. Carried to its logical limits, it entails a total transformation of the created order, "a new heaven and a new earth." By adopting this symbol as an expression of what his actions mean,

Jesus in effect declares himself the universal agent of redemption. It is no great leap, therefore, for the church to make the same identification by incorporating his story within the larger "story of salvation." If what he does is a manifestation of the intention exhibited in that story, then he himself is a part of the story. And since the story has universal implications, so must he also.

This is not to take away from the particularity of the story or the particularity of Christ as the principal agent in the story. It is, however, to suggest that particularity need not exclude universality, and that in this case the universality of the action helps to identify it as the action of God. It could even be argued that what makes Christ unique in addition to the perfection of his agency is the way in which he manages to combine universality and particularity. He is never more himself than when acting as the representative of others. His role as Redeemer is also his identity as a person. The two simply cannot be separated.

Together then miracle and prophecy serve to identify Jesus as the Christ. They do not do so in such a way as to constitute proof of his divinity, but they at least give some objectivity to the identification. It is not a purely private or subjective matter. There are criteria for identifying an action as the action of God, criteria consistent with the concept of agency. If in the end we find Christ's action inconceivable, it is not because he is less an agent than ourselves but because his agency is so immeasurably enhanced by his identification with God.

IDENTIFICATION AND VERIFICATION

When analytical philosophy first attacked theology it argued that reference to God could not be meaningful since there was no way of verifying the reference. Unless conditions could be given which would conclusively validate or invalidate theological assertions they must be assumed to be meaningless. Moreover the conditions which were allowed to count for verification were conditions of a narrowly empirical sort, that is to say, conditions having primarily to do with sense perception. Since then, the standards for verification have been loosened considerably, yet the verificationist principle of meaning persists. Many philosophers still assume that, unless it can be proven that God exists, it is not even meaningful to talk about him.

This is not a tenable position, however, for several reasons. In the first place, the concept of God is not the sort of concept that is susceptible to proof. Inasmuch as it has to do with a transcendent reality, it cannot be brought down to the level of straightforward empirical observation. It belongs to a different stratum of meaning than concepts for which empirical verification is relevant. Moreover, it has come increasingly to be recognized that even concepts which are much less problematical than the concept of God are not verifiable in the way that they were once thought to be. This is not simply because we lack the means to carry out the requisite tests, but because the concepts themselves are not sufficiently defined to permit us to say what would constitute conclusive verification. We know that certain evidence "speaks for" a particular assertion and other evidence "speaks against" it, but we cannot say what would put an end to doubt.

What makes for this inconclusiveness is a feature of empirical concepts which Waismann calls "open texture."[15] It is to be distinguished from vagueness in that it does not involve a fluctuating or imprecise use of terms, but rather an essential incompleteness. There is always the possibility of the emergence of something new and unexpected which would cause us to revise or expand the concept. "Every description stretches, as it were, into a horizon of open possibilities." But if this is true of most empirical concepts, as Waismann thinks it is, it must surely be true of concepts relating to God. Given the universality of God's action and the originality with which he acts, any statement concerning his intention, any attempt to say what he is up to, is sure to be incomplete. The possibilities in respect to God's action are literally inexhaustible.

But at least this is not a feature peculiar to theological concepts. The fact that other concepts are similarly incomplete suggests that it is not an insurmountable obstacle to overcome. We are able to communicate meaningfully in ways that do not meet the standards of scientific exactness for we do it every day. In fact, some of our most meaningful communications are of this sort. They are not so vague that we cannot act upon them, yet neither are they so exact that they can be conclusively verified. They are meaningful without being verifiable.

But then if we cannot insist upon verification as a requirement for meaning what about identification? One of the more important dis-

15. Friedrich Waismann, *Logic and Language*, ed. Antony Flew (Oxford: Basil Blackwell, 1955), vol. 1, p. 119 [125].

tinctions which has arisen in the course of recent discussions concerning the problem of meaning is the distinction between identification and verification.[16] Though it is not always stated with precision, it comes down to a distinction between what can be referred to meaningfully and what can be shown to be the case. Identification requires that we be able *to tell what we are talking about* so others can understand us and make some judgment about the truth or falsity of what we are saying. It leaves open the question of how it would be established that what we were saying is true. It is, therefore, a less austere and stringent requirement, yet at the same time a more basic one. Identifiability, as contrasted with verifiability, is a prerequisite for any sort of meaningful communication between persons. If I have no way of finding out what another person is talking about, I can hardly be said to understand him. He might as well be speaking a foreign language.

Identifiability has, of course, been a central concern of our discussion from the beginning. Our objective from the outset has been not to prove the existence of God but to establish the meaningfulness of talk about God. In order to do so we found it necessary to show how it is that God is identified. We began with identification of a very general sort—placing the concept of God in relation to other concepts. While this does not yield an exact determination of the concept, it does serve to indicate what we are talking about. The word *God* is not so vague that it can mean anything a person might want it to mean. Thus, where the primary model is personal agency, God is located on a scale of activity ranging from "sheer movement" to "deliberate choice." His agency is distinguished from all others by the perfection, the scope and efficacy, the freedom and self-determinacy with which he acts. He is, in other words, not limited as other agents are. His agency can serve as the basis for every other agency.

The difficulty with this form of identification is that it is so general. It does not allow us to speak of God's action with any sort of particularity. In the case of other agents we are able to distinguish something they have done from something they have not done. We are even able in most cases to give a neutral description of their action, in the sense

16. See especially Strawson, *Individuals: An Essay in Descriptive Metaphysics* (London: Methuen, 1961), pp. 15 ff. [2 ff.]. For a helpful discussion of this distinction with particular reference to Strawson's use of it, see Don Locke, *Myself and Others: A Study in Our Knowledge of Other Minds* (New York: Oxford University Press, 1968), pp. 132 ff.

that we are able to describe their bodily movements without regard to what they mean. This is not possible in the case of God.[17] There is no merely bodily description which can be given of his action, nor any way to refer to his action apart from reference to his intention. God, we have said, is that Agent whose intention is identical with his action.

Identification, if it remains at this level of generality, is necessarily going to be quite thin. It is going to lack the specificity and particularity necessary to make it practically meaningful. If the concept of God is to be more than a theoretical construct we need some way of identifying his specific intention for us as agents. In the Christian tradition, the way in which this is done is by reference to Christ. In the action of Christ, it is believed God has made himself bodily present. He has identified himself personally with specific historical events. Thus, the element of bodiliness which in our initial analysis seemed so crucial to the concept of agency, yet which was bound to be inapplicable to God, is reinstated after all. There is a sense in which God is a bodily agent. It is, however, a very special sense, wholly dependent upon the initiative of God. He is bodily identifiable because he has chosen to act in a bodily way toward us, not because he is in principle a bodily agent.

The bodiliness of Christ's action, we have argued, serves to give identifiable particularity to God's action. It enables us to say with some sort of definiteness and specificity what it is that God intends. But the question then arises as to just what sort of identification this is. Strawson, in his discussion of identification, distinguishes two basic types: "story-relative" and "demonstrative" identification. The one is identification relative to what someone says (without any independent reference); the other concerns what can be sensibly discriminated.[18] From what we have been saying up till now it would appear that identification of God is strictly story-relative, for we have ruled out demonstrative identification in any ordinary sense by denying that God is bodily limited. Only to the extent that he may be said to identify with the action of Christ can he be said to be demonstratively identifiable, and even then we are dependent upon a story (the Gospel story, the biblical story of salvation, the church's continuing

17. Compare Donald Evans, *The Logic of Self-Involvement* (New York: Herder & Herder, 1969), pp. 249–52.
18. Strawson, *Individuals*, pp. 18–19 [5–6].

story). For it is only in relation to this story that Jesus is identifiable as the Christ, the embodiment of God's intention for us. There is no possibility of simply pointing to God, certainly no way of "sensibly discriminating" God.[19] It would seem to be a foregone conclusion, therefore, that identification of God is story-relative.

Yet if this is so, it poses a serious problem for the believer since implicit in much that he says is the assumption that he is not simply telling a story but making a claim of fact. He means to say something about what is actually so, and we seriously misconstrue what he is saying if we suppose otherwise.[20] Thus, when a person speaks of God, he is very often expressing a hope that things will turn out in a certain way. This hope would mean nothing if he did not believe that something or other was so (for instance, that God has an intention for man that goes beyond anything presently experienced). Whether or not this belief is well founded, it is at any rate a constitutive element in what is said. It is a factor to be reckoned with in any assessment of the meaning of religious assertions.

Still we might agree that Christological identification of God is story-relative, if it were understood what sort of story this is and how it functions. It is, first of all, a paradigmatic story. By that I mean a story which fulfills a normative function in our discourse. It is not simply one story among others, the illustration of some universal truth. It is the standard by which truth of a certain sort is judged, the criterion for saying what God is doing at any given time. Of course, it is not so for everyone, but only for those who participate in the form of life in which this story is normative. Only in that context can it be said to have paradigmatic significance. Yet for those who do participate in this form of life, it is more than just a story; it is a "rule of faith."

As a paradigm of faith, it is interpretive of what is going on in the world. That is the other thing that needs to be said. Otherwise we might suppose that because it is a story it bears no relation to the larger world of events in which we all participate. In fact, its primary function as a story is to interpret this larger world of events, to provide insight into our situation as agents. It does so by identifying God's intention in such a way that we can then recognize his action

19. Compare Ronald Hepburn, *Christianity and Paradox* (New York: Pegasus, 1966), pp. 60 ff.

20. See John Wisdom's essay, "Religious Belief," *Paradox and Discovery* (New York: Philosophical Library, 1965), pp. 43 ff.

elsewhere. There is, we might say, a "family resemblance" among God's actions in various situations—and Christ's action is the key to discerning that resemblance. That is not quite correct, though, since in virtue of the normative role which his story has for us we cannot really distinguish his action from God's. What he does *is* what God does. We might rather say, therefore, that God's way of acting in the world is to extend to us all the one action of Christ. This action is unique in that it does not terminate with the agent's death but continues into the present. It is also unique in the significance it has for us—but we shall want to say more about that later.

For now the important thing to realize is that the story has empirical relevance: it cannot be treated simply as a self-contained entity. This may not constitute demonstrative identification of the sort that Strawson thinks is important, but at least it means that the identification is something other than merely story-relative. It does not concern simply what is said but also what can be observed here and now. It concerns an action in which we all more or less participate, though in virtue of its transcendent character an action which we frequently misperceive or fail to identify. That is why the story is so important: it enables us to make the identification. It says what God is doing here and now.

But then are we saying that it is only within the Christian community that this way of speaking about God is intelligible? Are we not, after all, treating religion as a kind of "private language"? Its meaning may not be limited to a single individual, but it does seem to be limited to a single community. This, however, is not the case. For we have been at pains to show that this way of speaking meshes with our other ways of speaking. It is an extension of the language of personal agency to speak of God as Agent, not a departure from it. Even the "criteria of ultimacy," by which Christ's action is identified as the action of God, belong within this framework. It is not necessary to do violence to the concept of agency or the fabric of interrelated agencies in order to speak of God's action in the world. The Christ-story is in principle intelligible to anyone who understands himself as an agent.

That still leaves open the question whether this story is to be judged "true" or not. At least though it is communicable: its meaningfulness is not confined to a single community. If it is judged true, it will be because it gives coherence to our experience—it makes sense of what is happening to us and through us—and also because it gives direction and significance to our action—a reason for doing what we do. Call that, if you will, a "subjective judgment." It is in any case open to corroboration by others and therefore not private. What is more it is the sort of judgment we should expect to find in religion, where what is at issue is a form of life, a total way of being in the world, not simply an objective matter of fact.

6. GOD AND OURSELVES

The story of Christ, as it has been understood within the Christian tradition, is more than simply the remembrance of someone's past deeds or the fragment of some ancient myth: it is God's personal word to man, a declaration of his intention for man. As such it affects a person's understanding of himself and his situation as an agent. It has practical implications.

Up till now we have been principally concerned with the logic of the concept of God, but we must also reckon with its more existential meaning. If, as we have said, religion articulates a form of life, we cannot presume to have fully understood one of its central concepts until we have shown how it bears upon that form of life. The necessity for drawing out the practical implications of one's theology is made all the more urgent by the present social crisis. For there is reason to think that many of the problems of Western society are rooted in its belief structure—which in turn derives largely from Christianity.

Thus, having considered various models for God, we need now to correlate these models with actual patterns of religious life. We need to see what sort of difference they might make for our understanding of ourselves and our situation as agents.

ALIENATION OR ANOMY?

We might expect that there would be no problem relating divine agency to human agency since it was in relationship to a concept of ourselves as agents that we initially formulated our concept of God. But that would be to suppose a deductive system, which we simply do not have when we are operating on the borderline between language strata. Whatever relationship there is between our conception of ourselves and our conception of God, it is not a relationship of entailment.

The problem is further complicated by the fact that the language we use to speak of God is non-literal. The concepts and images by which we relate ourselves to the transcendent are borrowed from other areas of discourse and qualified to give them a religious meaning. In drawing out their implications, we have a temptation to reduce their meaning to a level we can understand, but that is a temptation we must resist; otherwise we will have defeated our purpose. We will have distorted the relationship we set out to explicate.

In terms of the model of personal agency, there are basically two directions in which the distortion might go: alienation and anomy. If we stress the ultimacy of God's agency, we may be led to deny any reality to human agency. After all, if God intends all that he does and does all that he intends, what is there left for human agency to do? What scope is there for human action if God's action is absolute? Mankind may retain a semblance of freedom, but it can be no more than a semblance since any real choice on man's part would limit the efficacy of God's choice. If God intends what we shall be, he must intend what we shall do. What we do, therefore, is not our own doing but his. We are not agents in any real sense; we are patients. He is the potter; we are the clay. The world of which we are a part is one great artifice, and he is the unseen artisan.

This is basically Sartre's view of religion. It is a form of alienation with God as the Ultimate Alien. Unless man's freedom is grounded in himself so that it is he who makes himself and not some other, he is not free. He is not his own man. By intending for man God invests him with an identity not of his own determination—an alien identity. Man becomes, as it were, a stranger to himself. Of course, it is not only God who may do this. Others also try to impose an identity on him. Society lays down roles for him to fulfill. Individuals who feel they have some special claim on him (parents, employers, magistrates) dictate what he shall do and in that way limit what he shall be. Anyone is a potential source of alienation; yet no one so much as God, for his will can neither be evaded nor transcended. His freedom is man's necessity.

The argument is a familiar one advanced both by existentialists in the interests of self-authenticity and by sociologists on behalf of a greater sense of responsibility for the social order. For it is as reasonable to suppose that God determines the social system in which we have our identity as social selves, as it is to suppose that he determines our individual choices. Either way we are alienated from our own center of choice and self-determination. Yet it is possible to go in the opposite direction and to see in God's agency the legitimation of our own.

Freedom is such an elusive thing. If it is grounded solely in ourselves and our social institutions, what assurance have we that it will endure? How much more secure it would be if it were grounded in God. After all, why suppose that God cannot communicate his freedom to man? According to the biblical account of creation, man is created in the image of God. If God is free, this must mean that man is free. Being in the likeness of God, he must have the capacity to decide for himself what he shall be and what shape he shall give to his world. As God is transcendent, man is transcendent.

According to this view, belief in God should be the very opposite of alienating: it should be liberating. Through identification with God in his transcendent freedom, man is lifted out of the necessity which the world imposes on him. He is no longer subject to an alien order; he makes his own order. Nature is the name we give to this alien order, but man is not a part of nature. He is "above" nature, and therefore in a position to dominate it, to subject it to his will, to make of it what he will. But by the same token, he has no fixed set of relationships within which to identify himself, no overarching structure of meaning with which to orient himself. He is radically on his own in a world without any intrinsic order or purpose. That can be a terrifying prospect.

It can also be a license for oppression and domination. With no external restraints and even a certain justification for doing as we will, we may be led to treat others as mere objects and the world as of no intrinsic worth. We may come to suppose that our freedom, like God's, knows no bounds. If the alienated man is one who has forgotten that he is an agent, the anomic man is one who supposes that he is sovereign. He forgets that there are agents other than himself and that his action is necessarily contingent upon their action.

Failure to appreciate the context of our actions and the tendency to set ourselves above other agents, especially those belonging to the natural world, has no doubt contributed to the present "ecological crisis." If we credit no order beyond what we ourselves give to things we are unlikely to acknowledge a constraint upon our actions from others or endeavor to fit our actions to the requirements of nature. It should come as no surprise, then, to learn that we have so disrupted the natural environment that it threatens no longer to support us or that we have so undermined the fabric of trust on which society is based that it is in danger of collapse. This is simply the outcome of a more general presumptiveness.

It is ironic though that belief in a transcendent God should lead to both conclusions: anomy and alienation. There must be a flaw in the argument somewhere—either that or a basic misunderstanding. From the point of view of our earlier discussion the problem would seem to be a failure to accept the paradox of two agents. The conception of God as Ultimate Agent involves both the agency of God and the agency of the creature at different levels. Neither a view which denies agency to the creature on the grounds that God alone is sovereign nor one which conflates the two on the assumption that they are indistinguishable can be said to do justice to the paradox. Both the critics of the left and the critics of the right assume that all action-talk must belong to the same level of discourse. They do not suppose that it is possible to view human agency within the context of divine agency without one displacing the other.

Still there may be some point to their criticism. It requires a certain religious austerity to live with bare, unmitigated paradox. Kierkegaard seems to have been able to manage it, yet few since have been willing or able to go the whole way with him. Even Barth, after an early foray in that direction, tempered his attack on the "accommodators" and began to lace his theological discourse with a variety of metaphors for the relationship of God and man. Certainly the biblical literature is rich in images and metaphors for the relationship. It is as though, having realized the impossibility of speaking literally of the way in which God acts in the world, the biblical community felt no constraint in heaping image upon image. Within the general framework of agency, all manner of different ways were found for suggesting how God's action relates to our own—and this undoubtedly accounts for much of the affective power of biblical speech.

The biblical story is nothing if not a story of God's direct dealings with man. Though it is never forgotten that God is God, and therefore a profound and ultimately impenetrable mystery, it is assumed that whoever or whatever God is he is a power to be reckoned with. There can be no question of divorcing God from the world or divesting him of the qualities that would relate him concretely to man. If this way lies anthropomorphism, the biblical community was prepared to run that risk rather than flounder on the shoals of abstraction and irrelevance. We would do well to follow their lead.

However, rather than go directly from models to images, I would suggest an intermediate stage, one which involves a further specification of the model. Since our primary model is agency, that would mean a specification of the different ways in which God's agency might be thought of as related to our own. There is no obvious term for this intermediate stage of analysis, but I would suggest speaking of motifs within the larger story of God's dealings with man. The different motifs bring out different aspects of the relationship, while their interweaving corrects for misleading tendencies in each. If there is no literal way of specifying the relationship, we may compensate, as in the case of the concept of God, by balancing one motif off against another.

Not only that but we shall try to incorporate into these different motifs other ways of speaking of God than simply as Agent. The objections brought against the traditional view of God need to be taken seriously for they suggest real limitations in the concept of agency as a theological model. It ought not to stand alone; it needs to be supplemented by other models, other ways of speaking. The two models which we shall employ in this qualifying role are those of elusive subjectivity and communal identity discussed earlier. If they cannot serve as primary models (for reasons already given), they may nevertheless serve as qualifying models. This will still not provide us with a literal understanding of the relationship between God and ourselves; but it should at least help to dispel some of the more common forms of misunderstanding.

ECOLOGICAL MOTIF

Let us begin with the point of view of the environmentalist who says that Christianity has spiritualized man beyond all recognition by abstracting him from his natural setting in the world. You cannot properly understand man in isolation from his fellowman, and neither can you understand him in abstraction from the natural world. Nature is a vast complex of interconnected systems. Though each one has a certain integrity and life of its own, none is entirely independent or wholly self-sufficient. The removal of any one of these systems alters the ecological balance and affects other systems, however indirectly. Man is no exception to this rule. Whatever he does he does through interaction with other agents—personal and natural. Whatever relationship he has with God, he has within this wider network of relationships.

This viewpoint is not so alien to Christianity as one might at first suppose. In spite of a certain tendency to abstract man from the world, the weight of tradition, particularly biblical tradition, has never been on the side of a purely spiritual identity for man. The Hebraic conception of man is solidly on the side of bodily identity, and it is this bodiliness which places man squarely within the confines of nature and the interplay of agencies which make up the natural world. As a bodily agent I am engaged with other agents—members of my community, creatures of the natural world, inanimate forces of various kinds. They limit what I can do, but they also make possible many of the things I do. Thus, I may join with others of my community in a common venture, such as agriculture or war; I may harness the energies of certain animals to perform tasks beyond my own power; I may utilize natural processes, such as the heat emitted by the sun or the force generated by falling water, to enhance my capacity as an agent. I need not suppose that all of these systems are agents in the same sense that I am. They certainly do not act with intention and may not even exhibit purposiveness; yet they are active, and in a certain sense active of themselves. Their activity must, therefore, be reckoned with in any acting I do—whether as a limit to my own action or as a support.

Critics of Christianity from the point of view of ecology frequently fix upon the first chapter of Genesis, in which man is given dominion over the creatures of the earth, to support their view that Christianity is non-ecological. Yet it is significant that even before man is spoken of God is credited with having built up a vast complex of interacting systems declared to be good in their own right. It is not claimed that God established these systems simply for man's benefit, much less that he manipulates them to suit human convenience. Nor is it asserted that man can act in total disregard or defiance of them. Nature has an integrity and autonomy of its own. Man ignores the natural world at his peril.

In their preoccupation with personal salvation, Christians have often forgotten that redemption takes place within the context of creation. Creation in turn is not a momentary occurrence. It is the continuing action of God whereby he establishes and maintains the world as a going concern. The creatures of his will are not mere phases of his activity. They are invested with an identity of their own. The degree of autonomy and self-determination they enjoy is various —ranging all the way from the sheer movement of electrons to the highly self-conscious, deliberative action of persons. In between we encounter all manner and degree of organization. If we are wise, we will take the measure of these different activity-systems and fit our actions to them. For to act in sovereign disregard of all that is going on around and within us would be the height of foolishness. It could only lead to frustration and futility. Whatever the form of God's redemptive action, it cannot be such as to totally disregard the larger context of creation.

If we are to speak meaningfully of God's purpose for us, we must see that purpose as set within a larger context. For whatever the purpose, it must be a purpose for us as agents and as agents we are situated within a larger field of activity. The multiplicity of activity-systems with which we interact must be taken with full seriousness or our own action, even with the best of intentions, will come to naught. Another way of putting it would be to say that God can only enhance our action in relation to the action of other agents. That is because our very identity as agents is bound up with theirs. We cannot act alone and still be the persons we are. If God is to redeem us, he must in some sense redeem the whole cosmos.

What we have called the "ecological motif" is a way of assuring that the action of God will have universal scope. It is also a way of making certain that the relationship we have with God will not preempt or dissolve all other relationships. Having affirmed the importance of communal identity earlier, we are not about to deny it now. Rather we want to say that the relationship with God is implicit in our other relationships. Being related to God does not take us out of the world, but instead puts our relationship to the world in a different light. Inherent in all our dealings with the world, there is an underlying responsibility to God. He is engaged with us even as we are engaged with one another.

Among contemporary theologians, none has developed this idea more profoundly or with greater consistency than H. Richard Niebuhr. His conception of the "responsible self" places the identity of the person squarely within a network of relationships, yet not in such a way as to exclude relationship to God. On the contrary, he insists that the self can be an integrated self, amidst all the forces and events which act upon it, only if there is "One beyond the many" with whom it can interact. If I have my identity exclusively in relation to the multiplicity of forces and agents with whom I interact, I am not one but many. Only as I acknowledge in trust "that whatever acts upon me, in whatever domain of being, is part of, participates in, one ultimate action, then though I understand nothing else about the ultimate action, yet I am now one."[1]

It is sometimes supposed that if nothing determinate can be said about an action it can have no practical implications; yet, as Niebuhr shows, this is not so. An action whereby "I am" and "I am who I am" independently of the many roles I play and the many systems of action to which I respond is no matter of indifference. It can mean the difference between a unitary self and a fragmented self, an enduring self and a self which is only a momentary phase in a process.

What is more it can make a difference for how we place ourselves in relation to others. We always view the actions upon us in terms of some larger whole—a social group, a political process, the natural environment. If the context within which we operate is quite small, our capacity for action will be limited. If I understand everything in terms of my family, for instance, I will not understand much that is going on around me. I will not feel much a part of things. On the other hand, if I see myself in relation to One who acts in all things, I will have a quite different response. I will see those with whom I interact as belonging to "one universal society which has its center neither in me nor in my finite cause but in the Transcendent One," the One beyond the many; and that cannot help but affect my attitude toward them.[2]

It will affect it in at least two ways, according to Niebuhr. In the first place it relativizes the claims of other communities to which I belong and qualifies the loyalty I may feel for them. That includes not only the family, race, or tribe, to which I may be inclined to give my first allegiance, but the human community as such and even the biosphere. A radical conception of divine agency relativizes every system of finite agency and frees the person from every sort of totalitarianism. At the same time, however, it universalizes the responsibility we feel for others than ourselves. If we belong to a universal community, then we can with consistency no longer retain parochial loyalties. Though we cannot be responsible for everyone, we must not set arbitrary limits to our responsibility. None of the agencies with

1. H. Richard Niebuhr, *The Responsible Self* (New York: Harper & Row, 1963), p. 122.
2. Ibid., pp. 123–24.

which we interact can be looked upon as purely instrumental to our ends. The manifold systems of action which encompass us and engage us must be seen as having their own integrity and their own intrinsic worth.

The ecological motif in this way meets the principal objection of the environmentalists. It corrects the tendency toward anthropocentricism which they see in Christianity. Yet it does so by relying heavily upon the qualifying models of elusive subjectivity and self-in-community. God as the One beyond the many, the creative ground of all that is, stands so outside of the processes of nature and history that it is difficult to see what sort of difference he makes. Is it possible even to speak of interaction within this frame? Though Neibuhr talks of "response in trust or distrust to the radical act of the self's and the world's creation," it is an odd sort of response that has existence itself as its object. It is more like a basic attitude or orientation of the self toward the world that he is speaking of—one that counts God in as an active presence in the world. In order for us to respond actively to that presence, it must manifest some particularity. God must be more than simply "the One beyond the many." But that means we must adopt a different motif, a different way of conceiving the relationship between God and ourselves.

DIALOGICAL MOTIF

A recurrent criticism of religious discourse is that it is vacuous: it adds nothing to our knowledge of the world. Scientific generalization, historical reconstruction, even psychological explanation is unaffected by what religion has to say. Everything goes on as before. But if this were so, we could just as well dispense with it. A language which does not affect in any significant way our understanding of ourselves and our world is not a language which can have very much meaning for us.

What we have called the ecological motif is particularly vulnerable to this line of criticism. Although it would not be entirely fair to say that it leaves everything as is, that is something of the effect it has. It does not directly challenge other systems of explanation, such as science and history, but instead opens up a different dimension of meaning altogether. It does not add some additional item to experience, so much as it places the whole of experience within an inclusive frame. What difference it does make would seem to be of a highly subjective sort—confirmation of one's selfhood, relativization of one's loyalties, a sense of the underlying unity in all things.

This may simply be the way it is with religion, and if so we should acknowledge it. But it is not the impression one gets from biblical literature. There it would seem that God's presence does make a difference: it affects the outcome of events. He is the Creator, and therefore the presupposition of everything that is, but he is also an Agent whose intention has some direct bearing upon us as agents. What he does can actually alter our situation as agents and cause us to act differently from how he would otherwise. In fact, one might conclude from the biblical writings that man's history is one of continual interaction with God. His intention makes a difference and that difference is reflected in the course of events. Far from being vacuous, the biblical way of speaking of God is altogether too objective and interpersonal for most contemporary tastes. It seems to border on the mythological.

There are, of course, different senses of mythological, but what we have in mind principally is Bultmann's view that any language which "objectifies" God is mythological. To speak of God as one cause among others or of his action as though it were an objective occurrence is mythological. This way of speaking is both scientifically and religiously unacceptable. It is scientifically unacceptable because it is not subject to the verification procedures of science; it cannot be brought under general laws of explanation. It is religiously unacceptable because it does not do justice to the transcendence of God; it brings his action down to the level of ordinary occurrences.

This would seem to put us in a bind: either we retain the element of transcendence and sacrifice the concreteness and particularity of the biblical way of speaking or we run the risk of absurdity in adopting a way of speaking that is neither religiously nor scientifically acceptable. But perhaps there is a way out of this dilemma if we recall our earlier discussion of the word of God. That way of speaking about God did not lack concreteness or particularity, yet neither did it seem to have the objectivity or impersonality which Bultmann criticizes. It is, in fact, an approach which he himself adopts in his "demythologizing" interpretation of the New Testament. An assertion is not mythological, he thinks, as long as it takes the form of direct address and elicits from the hearer an appropriately personal response.

We need to consider, therefore, alongside the ecological motif, what

I would call the "dialogical motif." It has to do with the intention of God as it is directed specifically to us as agents. That intention may manifest itself in the situation before us or in reflection upon what we ourselves are doing; but in any case there will need to be some identifying word. We cannot expect simply to read God's intention off the course of events. Within the Christian tradition, the identifying word by which we are enabled to speak concretely and particularly of God comes from the biblical witness to Christ. By articulating for us, in word and deed, the intention of God, he puts us into a dialogical relationship with God. He constitutes, in the words of Austin Farrer, "the visible unity" of God's operations in the world.

Earlier we discussed the features of Christ's story which give it the character of ultimacy. Now we need to consider how it bears upon our situation as agents, what sort of practical implications it has. That could provide insight into the grounds for saying that this story is the word of God—a kind of pragmatic justification—but for now our principal interest is simply in drawing out the implications of this way of speaking for our self-understanding as agents. What specifically does the word of Christ have to say to us as agents, and how does this fit into a more general understanding of agency?

The first thing to be said is that the word of Christ is a word of judgment. This may come as a surprise since up till now the emphasis has been upon the compassionate, accepting nature of Christ's ministry, yet it is actually implicit in the claim that he is the embodiment of God's intention *for us*. If he sets before us an intention which God has for us, he subjects us to a transcendent norm. If we accept that norm we are judged by it. There is simply no getting around that implication.

Judgment need not, however, entail condemnation. It may simply be a matter of determining what is right in a particular situation. If we accept the principle that no "is" implies an "ought," we cannot simply infer from a state of affairs what is the right thing to do.[3] Some normative considerations must be brought to bear upon the situation. In the light of certain norms, the situation will appear to require one course of action rather than another. In this sense, especially, Christ's word constitutes a judgment.

3. This contention derives from Hume and is widely accepted in contemporary discussion of ethics. It has been disputed, as in John Searle's article, "How to Derive 'Ought' from 'Is,'" *Philosophical Review*, vol. 73 (1964), but for the purposes of argument I will assume its basic validity.

Consider, for instance, the parable of the Good Samaritan. It sets before us a standard of responsibility in relation to others. It says, in effect, that others have a claim upon us—especially those in need—and this claim is immediate and unconditioned. In the story, the injured man represents this claim. It is implicit in his wretched condition, his battered body, his unconscious state. His wounds fairly cry out for attention—but only for those who see him as a neighbor. To the priest and the Levite the situation is mute: it makes no claim that they can see or will acknowledge. The Samaritan by responding to the needs of the man in distress makes explicit the claim that such persons have upon us. He puts the situation of the needy in a new light. Similarly, Jesus by his responsiveness to others articulates their claim upon us.

But that is not all. He radicalizes this claim. He invests it with ultimate significance. One way in which he does this is by making our very identity before God depend upon it. This is brought out quite powerfully in the parable of the Last Judgment, where we are told that we will be judged "in the last day" according to whether we fed the hungry, gave drink to the thirsty, or visited those who were in prison. These are not relative matters; they are matters of "life and death" for us. As if to drive the point home, Jesus commits his own life totally to others. He identifies completely with what has been called the "agapeistic way of life," so that not only the parables he tells but also the parable he enacts sets it forth as the norm.

It would not be correct to say that Christian belief simply means commitment to the agapeistic way of life, but this certainly is an important part of it. Anyone who takes the story of Christ in the way in which it is obviously meant must acknowledge that this way of life is set forth as the norm by which every situation is to be judged. This is not to say that it is a formula which provides ready-made prescriptions for action, but it is at least paradigmatic of the way in which a situation is to be viewed. It sets in relief certain aspects of the situation which might otherwise be obscure or ambiguous—and in that way makes us aware of our responsibility.

The word of Christ makes us aware of a dimension of meaning in our situation as agents; but it also makes us aware of a dimension of meaning in our own action. Consider the way in which Jesus interprets the Law. "You have heard that it was said to men of old, 'You shall not kill; and whoever kills shall be liable to judgment.' But I say to you that everyone who is angry with his brother shall be liable to judgment." It is sometimes supposed that in this way Jesus gives a subjective meaning to the Law. Yet anger can be just as objective, just as behavioral, as murder. The significance of Jesus' interpretation is that it extends the commandment against murder to include anger (as he also extends the commandment against adultery to include lust). The way that he does this is in effect to reidentify the act of anger so as to bring it under the admonition against murder. To speak angrily is to act with murderous intent; to look at a woman lustfully is to have already committed adultery with her in one's heart. The intention identifies the action; and since the intention is not in accord with the will of God, neither is the action.

The word of God, embodied in Christ, both enlarges and deepens our responsibility as agents. It puts us more in touch with others and more in touch with ourselves. At the same time, though, it reveals just how much we are at odds with ourselves. We are far from realizing the form of life for which we are intended. This, too, is an aspect of the judgment. We are at odds with our own essential nature and therefore not fulfilled as persons. By bringing a transcendent norm to bear upon the situation of the agent, Christ's judgment takes precedence over all other forms of judgment—both the judgment we make upon ourselves and the judgments which society makes upon us. This is not to deny the validity of these other judgments, but simply to recognize that they are not ultimate. Only the judgment of God is ultimate.

The reason for the ultimacy of God's judgment is the transcendent perspective he has toward our action. The perspective of society is to a certain extent transcendent, since it encompasses the interests and outlooks of many persons; yet it too is limited and subject to corruption. Besides, the judgments of society can be terribly impersonal. They seldom take account of the particularities of a situation in the way that the judgments of an individual do. It is, therefore, not inappropriate for an individual to set his judgment over against that of society, in other words, for him to regard his perspective as transcendent. This is especially true in the matter of interpreting his own action. He has a point of view toward his action which others do not have. That gives a certain authority to his judgment which others lack. On the other hand, they have an objectivity he lacks. So really both perspectives are needed. Yet transcending both is the perspective of

God. He judges our action with an immediacy and an objectivity which we lack, both corporately and individually. God, if he judges at all, judges from the perspective of his own ultimate intention.

Christ is the embodiment of that intention. His very presence constitutes a judgment—though not in the manner of an external authority. In confronting us with a transcendent norm, he obliges us to pass judgment on ourselves. We are not what we were intended to be. There is a hiatus between what we do and what we ought to do. Probably there is even a conflict between what we intend at one level and what we intend at another; for everyone intends in one way or another to be himself, and that is also what God intends. In contradicting the will of God, we contradict ourselves. What the word of Christ does is to expose that contradiction.

This could be a source of despair, and probably would be were it not for the words of forgiveness and promise which accompany this word of judgment. These "hopeful" words have the effect of opening up a situation which might otherwise seem closed and setting before the agent the prospect of a radically new life. He is not condemned to futility in all that he undertakes or so bound to his past decisions that he can never break free of them. Without ceasing to be responsible for what he does, he is enabled to act anew—and thereby enact a new identity for himself. Christ's word of forgiveness, together with his word of promise, affects the situation of the agent every bit as radically as his word of judgment.

Forgiveness is probably as distinctive an element in Jesus' message as anything we might name. It is the first word he speaks to the paralytic brought to him to be healed (only secondarily does he command him to take up his bed and walk); it is among the last words he speaks from the cross ("Father, forgive them for they know not what they do"). It is implicit in some of his most characteristic actions, such as his association with outcasts and his intercession on behalf of an adultress; and it is a frequent theme in his exhortations to his disciples ("If you forgive men their trespasses, your heavenly Father also will forgive you"). Probably, too, it was the single most shocking thing he did. For it apparently raised in many minds the question of blasphemy.

We might wonder, though, if forgiveness is really consistent with a message of judgment. Can Jesus at one and the same time hold men accountable for their actions, even widen the scope of their accountability as he seems to do, and release them from responsibility by granting them forgiveness? It would seem that he could do one or the other, but not both. That assumes, however, a certain view of judgment, namely, a punitive view. But that is not the way in which we have been speaking of judgment. We have not said anything about punishment, only about a normative understanding of one's situation as an agent. The judgment which Christ brings is a judgment as to the meaning of what we are doing. Forgiveness does not change that. On the contrary, it presupposes it. Until we acknowledge what we are doing, there is no hope of doing anything different.

The predicament of the agent is that he acts so often without the full knowledge of what he is doing, yet with the realization that he is responsible for what he does. Moreover, once he has initiated an action he cannot recall it. Action, particularly action involving others, is irreversible. The only remedy, therefore, is to begin again, to accept responsibility for what one has done and start over. But that is possible only if others permit it. No one can give himself a new beginning. He must first be released from the consequences of his action and accepted on a new footing; then he can think of starting over.[4]

Jesus gives persons this opportunity: he frees them from the consequences of their action so that they can begin anew. Take the case of the paralytic. It was thought at the time that sickness was the consequence of sin. Therefore, in order that people might know that he had the power to forgive sins, Jesus relieved the paralytic of his infirmity. He gave him the possibility of acting on a wholly new basis. In the case of the tax collectors and prostitutes whom he befriended, he did not hold their past actions against them. He accepted them into fellowship with himself in spite of their "social unacceptability." What he does in effect is to establish a relationship of mutuality in which the person is free to be himself.

But then what becomes of the assertion that a person has his identity in his action? If the person is accepted in spite of his action, does this not force a separation between person and act? In a sense, it does. We cannot simply equate personal identity with action if a relationship is possible which discounts action. It is important, therefore, that there be the complementary forms of identity discussed earlier: identity as subject and identity in community. Neither of these alternative

4. Hannah Arendt, *The Human Condition* (New York: Doubleday, 1958), pp. 212 ff.

forms of identity is strictly dependent on action; therefore they can provide the leverage necessary to spring a person loose from his action —if only so that he may act anew.

The identity that I have simply as a subject gives me a perspective upon my action. It enables me to pass judgment upon my own past behavior and, if I so choose, to launch forth upon a new course of action. Were it not for this elusive subjectivity, a person would be indistinguishable from his action. Strictly speaking, he would not even be the agent of his action, for that implies a certain subjectivity on his part. The problem with this form of identity is that it is so elusive, so difficult to pin down. I have difficulty thinking of myself as a subject apart from my actions. Yet it sometimes happens, through encounter with another, that I experience my subjectivity enhanced—and with it greater freedom to act. In that way I may be said to know myself both as subject and as agent.

Identity in community is somewhat different. It does not distinguish the person from his action, so much as it incorporates him within a larger totality in which his identity is not limited to what he does but includes what the community does. In accepting the ideals of a community and entering into relationship with those who make up the community, a person realizes an identity more inclusive and more continuous than what he has simply as an individual. It is more inclusive in that it takes in the actions of others, more continuous in that it does not vary with every variation in his own intention. Moreover, this same community can provide a sustaining nexus of relationships in which he is upheld and affirmed even when his action is at odds with the ideals of the community. In that way it too makes possible a new beginning for the person as agent. There is still judgment, but the judgment does not carry the implication of separation, isolation, inaccessibility to others. One is free to act anew in relationship to others.

Forgiveness, then, is a way of getting back of the action of a person to the identity he has simply as a subject, or as a subject in relationship to others. It is not, however, a denial of his agency. On the contrary, it is an explicit affirmation of his identity as an agent. So long as a person is bound to his past actions, he is not really free to define himself through his actions. Like the characters in Sartre's *No Exit*, he is condemned to live out an identity he has already chosen rather than choose a new one. Forgiveness is a way of saying that action is not a one time thing: persons can begin again, even in the midst of a situation they themselves helped to create. They can act freely.

But only with the help of others. Our transcendence as subjects is not so secure but that it requires the support of others. Only through mutual release from the consequences of past decisions and through mutual acceptance can we hope to sustain our identity as agents. That means that the resolution of our predicament as agents derives from the very condition which produced it, namely, the plurality of agents. As I am limited in what I can do by others and frequently remiss in fulfilling my responsibilities to others, it is nevertheless through others that I am enabled to make a new beginning. Their acceptance is the condition of my freedom.

But then what need is there for divine acceptance? Is there any reason to think that forgiveness must come from God? Hannah Arendt, in her book *The Human Condition*, gives one of the most incisive accounts of forgiveness in contemporary literature, yet she maintains that it is a human capacity and not dependent on God.[5] She considers Jesus an innovator in the area of action and the first to realize the necessity for forgiveness, but she does not think that even he made forgiveness contingent on God. He recognized it, instead, as a responsibility men owed to one another simply as men. Trespassing after all, is an everyday occurrence; it arises inevitably out of the web of relationships in which we stand as agents. Unless we are willing to forgive one another, we are in danger of destroying ourselves through a relentless process of revenge. It is not only right but necessary that we should forgive one another without waiting for the forgiveness of God.

There is a good deal to be said for this position. Certainly we ought not to suppose that forgiveness is the prerogative of Christians and that it must somehow depend upon hearing the word of Christ. On the other hand, we need not assume that just because it is something for which we are responsible, God is not responsible. The paradox of two agents for the same action permits ascription of an action both to God and to ourselves. Indeed, it is a characteristic of every action that it is both intended by God and by ourselves, though not always with the same meaning. Forgiveness would be an action in which our intention was in agreement with the intention of God.

5. Ibid., p. 215.

Arendt herself comments upon the originality inherent in forgiveness. It is the one reaction, she believes, "which does not merely re-act but acts anew and unexpectedly, unconditioned by the action which preceded it and therefore freeing from its consequences both the one who forgives and the one who is forgiven."[6] This makes it very much like action itself. It also makes it like the action of God. One of the distinguishing features of God's action, after all, is its originality. God is not conditioned by what has gone before. He intends with utter originality and spontaneity. In creating us "in his image," he communicates something of this capacity to us. Would it not be reasonable to expect that he should also renew that capacity in us? And what is forgiveness but a renewal of the capacity to act with originality, spontaneity, freedom? Arendt at one point speaks of action as "the one miracle-working faculty of man."[7] I would suppose that this could equally well be said of forgiveness.

Through the act of forgiveness we are enabled to share in God's transcendent perspective both on ourselves and on our world. In one sense, this takes us beyond the world, but in another sense it takes us into the world. We are freed from the necessity of retribution and enabled to act creatively in a way analogous to God's own creative act, yet we do so as human agents from within a nexus of relationships which define our place in the world. We are in, but not of the world.

By opening us up to this perspective on ourselves and our world, Christ's word of forgiveness like his word of judgment radically affects the situation of the agent. It is not the same situation when seen in relationship to God. Still this may not suffice to overcome what we have called the "predicament of the agent." For it is not only in respect to what he has done that he is limited, but in respect to what he is to do. No one in contemplating an action can be certain of the outcome. If he is at all realistic he knows that the outcome will depend as much on what others do as on what he himself does. The more interpersonal the action, the more this is true. But then how are we to fulfill our responsibility to others? If all our efforts are in vain—and we have no assurance they are not—what is the use of trying? The opportunity to make a new beginning would seem to be a meaningless concession.

6. Ibid., p. 216.
7. Ibid., p. 222.

Forgiveness by itself cannot overcome the limitations of finite agency. We have also somehow to reckon with the uncertainty of the future and our inability as agents to secure the outcome of our actions. Where we are dealing simply with inanimate agents or impersonal activity-systems, this is no great problem. For we are able to observe recurrent patterns, formulate general laws, and make predictions on the basis of these laws. Assuming that these systems can be isolated and their interaction with one another does not produce unexpected consequences, we may anticipate the future with reasonable certainty and act with confidence that something like what we intend will result from our action. But this is not possible where interaction is with agents like ourselves who also intend what they do and whose intentions may conflict with our own. In fact, the more freedom we attribute to them in the way of initiative, spontaneity, and originality, the greater the uncertainty.

The predicament of the agent is that he must take responsibility for actions whose outcome is uncertain and in any case not fully within his control. He must act into a future that is unknown and unknowable. Is there any remedy? Arendt thinks there is. Just as forgiveness is a way of "undoing" the past, promise-keeping is a way of "securing" the future. It does not enable us to predict the future with absolute exactitude, but it does enable us at least to anticipate the actions of others. Through the making and keeping of promises, persons bind themselves to a course of action which others can then count on. This serves, as she says, "to set up in the ocean of uncertainty, which the future is by definition, islands of security without which not even continuity, let alone durability of any kind, would be possible in the relationships between men."[8]

Both the capacity to forgive and the capacity to make promises presuppose a condition of plurality. No one can forgive himself and no one can feel bound by a promise made only to himself. If we were to try to do it for ourselves, it would lack reality. It would be like Wittgenstein's "private language," which means something only to the person himself and therefore can mean anything he wants it to mean. It quickly becomes illusory. What, for instance, would establish that a person had kept a promise with himself, that what he had done was in continuity with what he had promised to do earlier? Logically it may

8. Ibid., p. 213.

be conceivable, but practically it would mean extraordinary loneliness, ambiguity, and uncertainty. We need others to confirm that we have acted with consistency. In turn our willingness to fulfill a commitment greatly enhances their freedom to act by enabling them to anticipate our action. Promise-keeping, as Arendt says, enables persons "to dispose of the future as though it were present," and that constitutes an enormous, even "miraculous" enlargement of power.[9]

It is significant, therefore, that the word of Christ is not only a word of judgment and forgiveness, but also of promise. If this is not the most salient feature of his message, it is certainly a prominent element in it. Without it the hopes which Jesus aroused and the confidence toward the future which characterized his followers would be inexplicable. He gave men something to look forward to; he set before them a vision of what was to come; and he did so in such a way as to inspire their confidence.

Obviously it was not simply his own promise that had this effect, but a promise he made on behalf of God. When he said to the poor and destitute, "Blessed are you poor, for yours is the Kingdom of God," or to the downtrodden, "Blessed are you that weep now, for you shall laugh," he spoke for God. It was God who would secure the future for them, who would bring about their fulfillment. Likewise, when he proclaimed that the Kingdom of God was at hand, he meant that God was soon to bring it about that all would be subject to his rule. The promise which Christ conveys is God's promise for the whole of mankind.

In this sense, he is like the prophets who also make projections on behalf of God. Yet there is a difference. What Christ says, he also does. He enacts the promise which he so forcefully articulates. He realizes in his own person the very life which he sets forth as God's intention for man, so that no longer can it be thought of as merely an ideal. The trouble with most of our hopes is that they lack a sufficient grounding in reality. They are indistinguishable from wishful thinking. The same is true of the ideals we project for ourselves: they are often unrelated to the realities of our situation. This could also be true of Christ were it not for the fact that he actually does what he says. He embodies what he sets forth as the ideal.

The word of Christ would not be the word of promise that it is if it

9. Ibid., pp. 220–21.

merely expressed the intention of God. The enactment of this intention by God is an indication of his commitment to it. It is his pledge to see it through to completion. By his action in Christ, God binds himself to man and to his good. There are foreshadowings of this in the Old Testament—in the covenant with Abraham, the deliverance from Egypt, and the preservation of the faithful remnant—yet nothing like the depth of commitment implied in the crucifixion and made explicit in the resurrection. God has so committed himself to the realization of his intention for man that nothing, not even sin and death, can ultimately defeat it.

Does this word of promise stand by itself, isolated from the rest of experience? It might seem so when we reflect upon how much there is in experience which seems to count against it: untimely death, senseless brutality, dreams shattered by adversity, the efforts of good men come to naught. On the other hand, there is the capacity for transcendence which enables us to continue hoping in spite of frustration and defeat. Is this not a sort of promise built into the very structure of existence? It is, to be sure, not an unambiguous promise. But then what can we expect? Any promise implicit in existence-as-such is bound to be ambiguous. Moreover, the fact that we can speak of untimely death and frustrated good implies a conviction that things are not as they ought to be. There is a hiatus between the "is" and the "ought" which needs somehow to be closed, and which ultimately we might hope will be closed.

Still it is only a hope, and the sort of hope that borders on being simply a wish. The promise implicit in the nature of things does not have the backing of an event in which the gap between the "is" and the "ought" is actually closed as it is in the promise of Christ. Moreover, the promise implicit in our transcendence as agents is a largely inarticulate promise. It needs the word of Christ to make it explicit. This does not mean, however, that it is of no significance. Without it the word of Christ might well appear absurd and utterly unrelated to our experience. Only in conjunction with an intuitive sense of promise does the word of promise carry conviction.

Still it might be objected that the sort of promise of which we are speaking—an ultimate promise for the whole of mankind—so transcends the realm of probability as to be practically useless. What are we to do with a promise that takes in everything? Certainly if a person promises more than he can deliver, we do not put much stock in his promises. His word loses credibility. Yet is that not precisely what the church has done? It has put forth a promise so inclusive and far-reaching as to be beyond belief.

Miss Arendt makes an objection similar to this in her discussion of promise-keeping. She says that "the moment promises lose their character as isolated islands of certainty in an ocean of uncertainty, that is, when this faculty is misused to cover the whole ground of the future and to map out a path secured in all directions, they lose their binding power and the whole enterprise becomes self-defeating."[10] But does this apply to promises in a religious sense? It is obvious that, however powerful, an individual or an institution that promised to secure "the whole ground of the future" would lose credibility and would soon find that its claims were self-defeating, but that is because they are not made at the level of religious assertions. A promise such as Christ makes carries with it a different sort of expectation.

In the first place, it does not offer a literal description of the future. It sets forth a vision, a symbolic representation of what is to come. In the New Testament, the central image for the future is the Kingdom of God; but there are others, the New Jerusalem, the Wedding Feast, the Great Assize. What is important to keep in mind is that these are images. Literal representation of a future so inclusive and so definitive as to satisfy the religious longing is out of the question. Yet a symbolic representation is not without practical significance. For it can inspire hope, strengthen our expectations, and give a general direction to our actions. What a person believes about the future, even if it can be expressed only in symbolic terms, definitely makes a difference for what he does in the present.

To speak of the promise of God is in part to speak of a transcendent vision for man. But that is not all that it means. There is also implicit the assurance of an enduring relationship with God. Conceptually, this may be all that we can say, for when pressed our images of the future invariably prove elusive and indefinable. We really cannot say, except in relational terms, what a transcendent future would be like. Thus, Paul in his letter to the Romans contrasts the "spirit of sonship" with the "spirit of slavery" and argues that the whole creation groans in travail waiting for the "glorious liberty of the children of God." He will not speculate, though, as to what that consummation might be

10. Ibid., p. 220.

like, and in the end he simply asserts that nothing can separate us from the "love of God in Christ Jesus." Whatever shape the future may take, it will be a future with God. The relationship of love whereby God binds himself to us and us to him will endure, and that is the important thing.

We could go on with the dialogical motif, since there are undoubtedly other ways of analyzing the word of Christ than in terms of judging, forgiving, and promising, yet this should suffice to show the basic structure of this way of speaking. It is not a scientific, or even quasi-scientific way of looking at things; yet neither can it be said to leave everything as it is. The word of Christ radically affects the situation of the agent. It opens up a further dimension of meaning in the situation and points us beyond the situation to possibilities not yet realized. It definitely makes a difference for what people think and say and do.

Still it might be argued that this is a highly personal sort of difference. Is it not susceptible to a subjectivistic reduction? In speaking of the judgment of God, a person may simply be declaring his allegiance to a particular ideal. Reference to the forgiveness of God may come down to self-acceptance, while the so-called promises of God may be no more than expressions of hope. There would appear to be no objective reason for supposing that religious assertions do anything more than express a particular self-understanding or a particular world view. The transcendent referent might just as well be dispensed with.

The difficulty with this reductionist approach, however, is that the terms in question are all profoundly interpersonal. Judging, forgiving, and promising are all transactions between persons. No one forgives himself or makes a promise to himself except as the internalization of a dialogue he has with others. Moreover, it is generally not just anyone who can fulfill this function for us, but only what the sociologists call a "significant other." These are the persons with whom we stand in a particular relationship of dependence. They are the ones to whom we look for some definition of ourselves beyond what we are able to give ourselves. With their greater objectivity—hopefully combined with compassion—they can offer us a perspective on ourselves which we could not get in any other way.

By extension this would make God the ultimately Significant Other. His transcendent perspective would give him a knowledge of us like no other. In knowing him we would know ourselves in a more definitive way than through anyone else's knowledge of us, for we would be knowing ourselves in light of his ultimate intention for us. Whether or not we do what he intends is another matter. That is the difference between an enhanced agency and an agency that is ultimately self-defeating. The important thing, though, is that there is intention other than our own or our neighbors' that is definitive for who we are. Identity is not something we simply determine for ourselves or have determined for us by other persons; it comes also out of dialogue with the transcendent.

TELEOLOGICAL MOTIF

Probably no one has made more consistent or incisive use of the dialogical motif in recent times than Rudolph Bultmann. It has been his way of "demythologizing" the New Testament. Every significant theological statement is assumed to have the form of address and therefore to carry with it a reflexive meaning. "The Word of God is not a timeless statement but a concrete word addressed to men here and now."[11] It directs the hearer to God, but also puts him in touch with his true self. This is the deeper meaning concealed under the cover of mythology—a profoundly personal yet at the same time transcendent meaning.

The difficulty with this approach is that it can lead to an essentially inward transcendence. In spite of the otherness of the word which addresses me, I am ultimately thrown back upon myself. Moreover it is the self as "elusive subject" that is the final referent of Bultmann's existentialized theology, not the self as agent. The word of God calls me to a personal existence which is "beyond the visible world and beyond rational thinking." It summons me to decide but without giving specific direction to my decision. Authenticity is to be found primarily in the form of the decision rather than its content. To be sure I am called to decide in relation to the neighbor and as a Christian called to act out of love for the neighbor, yet there is very little sense of being part of a larger society or engaging in long-range projects of the sort which would give content to a decision. In addition, there is a problem of continuity. According to Bultmann, I decide myself anew in every moment on the basis of immediate encounter with the tran-

11. Rudolph Bultmann, *Jesus Christ and Mythology* (New York: Charles Scribner's Sons, 1958), p. 79.

scendent Other. As long as that Other is thought of simply as Subject, we do not have much to go on in forming for ourselves a sense of continuing identity. Without a community and without commitment to long-term goals, the self would seem to be existent only in the moment.

This has led critics of Bultmann to take up a theme which he neglects but which is of unquestioned biblical authenticity, the theme of the Kingdom of God.[12] Not only was it uppermost in Jesus' own teaching but it was an important element in the faith of Israel. It gives to that faith a social dimension which Bultmann's existential interpretation tends to obscure and a forward thrust which for all that he says about eschatology seems also to be lacking in his theology. As far as self-identity is concerned, it overcomes much of the isolation involved in existential decision-making by providing a context and direction for decision.

The theme of the Kingdom of God was very prominent in nineteenth-century thought, but went under something of an eclipse in the twentieth century. It has only recently been revived—in large part owing to the present social crisis. We have been made aware by a host of different problems (racism, technology, poverty, war) of the inadequacy of a purely individual piety. If the Christian faith is to have a transforming effect upon man, it must relate to him not simply as an individual but as a participant in a larger social order. Moreover, if it is to engage his participation in the formation of a new social order it must set before him a vision of what is to come, the new order that he is to help create. There is much that the biblical imagery of the Kingdom can contribute to such a task.

In the first place, it envisions man as having his identity in the company of other men. Israel is called to be the people of God, the company of the faithful. As such they are expected to embody in their corporate life a particular pattern of relationships, one characterized by such terms as justice, peace, mercy, love. Jesus in his teachings takes for granted the social meaning of the concept and presses home the need for personal commitment and for a sense of the immediacy of the Kingdom. Still it remains a social concept. The Kingdom of God is a form of life together, a corporate conception of human good.

The Kingdom is near, but it is not yet. That is a further feature of

12. See, for example, Wolfhart Pannenberg, *Theology and the Kingdom of God* (Philadelphia: Westminster Press, 1969).

Jesus' message. It looks forward to the ultimate fulfillment of God's purpose for man, but acknowledges that in the present this fulfillment is only a hope. That was, of course, true of the prophets also. They did not identify the Kingdom with any existent social arrangement. They envisaged a radical transformation of the total social order—and not the social order only, but the natural as well. The total context of man's life must eventually undergo transformation. For the present, we must do what we can to prepare for this great event. We must, as far as possible, anticipate the future.

The Kingdom of God is social and it is future, but above all it is God's. There can be no kingdom without a king. So whatever else the various images and parables of the Kingdom mean, they signify the rule of God. Jesus' message is characterized by an overwhelming sense of the imminent reign of God. The day is soon coming when God's power will be manifest and his sovereignty acknowledged universally. Demonic powers may reign for a time, but eventually all things will be subject to God's will, for he is the only true sovereign in the universe.

I have chosen to call this way of speaking the "teleological motif" because it conceives of God in terms of an all-embracing purpose. Just as we might think of the person's larger purpose as encompassing and giving meaning to his lesser purposes, so we may conceive of God as having a larger purpose for what he does. If we do not perceive it, it may be because the action is still in process, or because he has not chosen to reveal it, or simply because we are not very perceptive; but in any case the purpose is operative and will eventually come to fruition. If we can recognize it, we can cooperate with it. Otherwise we may find ourselves frustrated. Whether we know it or not, we will be working against the grain of reality.

Proponents of this way of speaking differ concerning how continuous or discontinuous this purpose is with all else that is going on in the world. The apocalyptic viewpoint, of course, is that it is radically discontinuous. When finally actualized it will mean the overturning of everything. We cannot possibly contribute anything to it; we can only await its coming and try not to set ourselves actively against it. The ameliorationist viewpoint would be that the divine purpose is everywhere present resisting evil and maximizing good. Because it is immanent in all things we can cooperate with it; we can subject our own purposes to this larger purpose and in that way make it our own. In the words of Paul, "all things work together for good with those who love God, who are called according to his purpose."

These are important differences, yet there is one thing that both views have in common and that is the conviction that man's fate is bound up with the cosmos in some important sense. The future will be determined not simply by my own choices or by impersonal powers beyond my control but by One whose purpose encompasses both myself and the cosmos. As a purposive being, man seeks to relate his purposes to what is going on in the universe. If he finds no logical connection—if he alone is purposive and everything else is mechanistically determined—he may despair of ever being at home in the universe, or he may question his own purposiveness; but the transcendent approach would be to look for a purpose originating outside of himself and the world, yet encompassing both. By relating to it, he would also be relating to the world.

But what about the disagreement between apocalypticists and ameliorists? How are we to resolve this difference? Their two positions would seem to be incompatible, yet they may have simply fixed upon two different aspects of intentional action. We may, after all, speak of intention in the future tense as a project yet to be realized or in the present tense as what the agent thinks he is actually doing. The first way of speaking focuses upon the outcome of the action, the person's long-term goal in doing whatever it is he is doing. The second way points up the meaning implicit in the action itself, the sense it has for the person doing it. The two ways of speaking need not be at variance; the overarching intent of the action may be precisely what it means to the agent. In that case, he would be a very integrated person. Since we have earlier argued that self-integration epitomizes divine action, there should be no need to separate present and future, as apocalypticists tend to do, or to dissolve the future into the present, as ameliorists are wont to do.

Still there may be an issue to be resolved in the fact that the one group tends to give all of the weight to God's agency leaving man with nothing but a passive role, while the other group envisages a cooperative arrangement whereby God and man together effect the course of events. There would seem to be a clear choice to be made here; and if we put it in just this way, there can be no question on which side we must come down. Man must act if he is to be. His identity is inseparable from his agency. So if God is to affirm him as a creature, he must affirm him as an agent. He cannot expect man to be entirely passive and remain man. On the other hand, God's agency is distinct from man's and prior to it. If the ameliorist has in mind to reduce God's agency to the sum total of creative activity, then his position too is unacceptable. There is, in other words, danger of dissolving the paradox in either direction. Yet assuming the distinctiveness of divine agency and the divine initiative in all things, we must conclude that the ameliorist has the better case. God's agency can no more be divorced from our own than it can be consigned to the future, since either way it would be meaningless to speak of it.

What is it, then, that God intends? Can we hope to give determinate meaning to this inclusive purpose? One approach would be to acknowledge that we cannot, and yet to maintain that it is meaningful to speak of God's having a purpose for us. His intention is that we should intend for ourselves. His intending, in other words, is the ground, source, or basis of our own intending. He means for us to be free and self-determining, but beyond that we cannot speak of his having a purpose for us. This is, however, a very thin notion of purpose. Unless we suppose God's purpose to have a specific shape and form, we had best give up a teleological motif. In fact, the view which treats God's purpose as simply the basis of our own purposing is really non-teleological. It makes sense to speak teleogically only if we suppose there to be a specific drift or direction to God's action in the world. That is certainly assumed by the image of the Kingdom, whether it is taken in an apocalyptic or an amelioristic sense. Yet can we posit an ultimate goal for God's action without undercutting the very freedom and agency of persons which was the starting point of our argument? To suppose that God has a specific intention for man and that what he intends he does would seem to leave the person with no choice. Sooner or later God will prevail.

But that depends on what the purpose is. Suppose it were such as to embrace a diversity of agents, each being himself yet contributing to a larger whole. That is surely not inconceivable, since something of the sort takes place wherever there is genuine community. Enforced conformity is not community, but neither is random interaction. Only as persons interact freely with one another on a basis of mutual respect (perhaps for the furtherance of some cause but possibly simply for the sheer delight of it) is there true community. It may be rare but it does happen, and when it does it is a foretaste of the Kingdom.

According to Jesus, what God intends is his Kingdom. According to Paul, what he accomplishes through Christ is the reconciliation of the world. There is no reason to suppose the two are different. What the imagery of the Kingdom depicts is a condition of ultimate reconciliation: the reconciliation of man with man and man with God. The action of Christ was an anticipation of this condition, a beginning of the new age. His love breaks down barriers to community—barriers of sickness and guilt, nationality and caste, self-righteousness and pride. Even death cannot separate him from those he loves and so his work goes on: the reconciling action of God continues.

Does this mean that there will eventually be an end to it? If we attribute an ultimate purpose to God, does this not mean that sooner or later his action will cease? So it might seem; yet we have said that his identity is in his action. How can it cease? The answer is, of course, that it cannot. What is more, it need not. Reconciliation is the sort of "end" to which there is no end. By intending our reconciliation, God intends for us a life of continuous interaction with one another in the spirit of love. The possibilities for such a life are literally inexhaustible.

That is our hope, yet we need not wait for it to come to us. Even now we are called to participate in this life, which is to say, in the reconciling work of God in the world. The teleological motif gains much of its significance from the fact that we can make God's intention our own. It need not be something external to us. If we intend what he intends we are one with him in his action.

It is not simply that we have the same goal in mind, that our purposes coincide, but that our action is rooted in his action so that he acts through us. The famous Pauline paradox, "I yet not I, but the grace of God with me," expresses this quite well.[13] The ascription of an action to God need not cancel out self-ascription; it can actually enhance it. For now I act in agreement with my own deepest aspirations. I am no longer at odds with myself. Earlier we spoke of the paradox of two agents. At that time it may have seemed like a very formal notion; but now that we have brought in the identifying word of God, we are in a position to give it some content. The action in which we participate when we identify ourselves with God is the

13. 1 Corinthians 15:10. For a further elaboration of this theme, see D. M. Baillie, *God Was in Christ* (New York: Charles Scribner's Sons, 1948), pp. 114 ff.

action of love. It is an action which reconciles us with both ourselves and others.

It calls for utmost trust and hope. For to act in love is to act in expectation of results we may never see. If however this love is from God, if in loving we participate actively in the life of God, then it is not in vain even if we do not see the results. God as the Ultimate Agent is the guarantor of all that he intends. He does not simply summon us to a course of action which he conceives to be good. He invites us to share in his action. Thus our action is given a meaning and an efficacy it would not otherwise have. The action of love, because it is also the action of God, is action with a future. In the words of Paul, it is the one thing that endures.

The teleological motif then is not simply an ethical motif. It is as religious, as much a matter of transcendence, as the other two. It simply relates us to the transcendent in a different way. All three motifs carry implications for action; all three bear upon our identity as agents; yet the teleological motif, more than any other, gives direction and meaning to our action. By placing our action within the context of God's action of love, it provides us with both a motive for action and an incentive to act. It gives transcendent meaning to our action.

THE GRAMMAR OF FAITH

The Christian story is built up through the interweaving of several distinct strands. In telling the story we seldom distinguish these different strands, yet in controversy with others (both within our tradition and outside of our tradition) we invariably find that we must play one motif off against another.

If we begin speaking in the teleological mode about God's overriding purpose for his creation and express the hope that ultimately his intention will prevail, we may be accused of denying any real agency to man. If God determines what man shall be, man does not determine himself: he is alienated from himself. In response, we may invoke the ecological motif—arguing that although God intends for every creature, what he intends is that the creature should be himself, which in the case of men and women means intending for themselves. Or we may appeal to the dialogical motif—maintaining that God in addressing us as Another confirms and even enhances our status as agents. Taken by itself the teleological motif may seem deterministic; qualified by the other two motifs it is not. The art of speaking religiously is the art of balancing off against one another these several ways of speaking.

What is true for the problem of alienation is equally true for the problem of anomy. An emphasis on the dialogical conception of man's relation to God may lead to the criticism that it separates man from the world, that it so defines his identity in I-Thou terms that it leaves no room for a meaningful relationship to the nonpersonal dimension of life. It may be necessary then to set over against this undoubted tendency in biblical thought the ecological motif with its conception of systems of action in interdependence with one another and the teleological motif with its conception of an overarching purpose reconciling the whole of creation.

On the other hand, were we to begin with the ecological motif, we could find ourselves confronted with two of the most persistent questions in any religious tradition, the questions of sin and death. The question of sin arises because the various action-systems in their mutual interaction invariably inflict damage on one another, and in the case of human agents will even purposefully injure one another. Death is a problem because within a framework simply of interaction every agent is limited and none endures. We act, but our action is continually being frustrated by the action of others and even the best of our actions do not generally have lasting results. A reply to both questions is to be found, however, in the other two motifs—not because they set aside the problem or answer it in its own terms but because they approach it from another perspective. The key to the dialogical motif is the personal relationship it posits between God and man. On the basis of this relationship sin is not denied or eliminated; persons are judged and forgiven. God's word of forgiveness is a principle of renewal in a world bent on its own destruction. His word of promise opens up a future for man beyond every limit, even that of death. It is a way of saying that man's relationship with the Ultimate is an enduring relationship. The teleological motif reinforces this hope by setting man's action within a trajectory of intention that overreaches the present and extends into the indefinite future. There is no end of possibilities for action because we participate in the action of God.

Of the three motifs, the one that is most closely tied to the intention-action model is the teleological motif: it is the one in which God is most clearly conceived of as Agent. To speak in this way about God and his action toward us is to call to mind Anscombe's notion of concentric descriptions for the same action. Just as a person's larger intention can encompass and support his lesser intentions, and even give meaning to them; so God's intention encompasses and supports us in what we do, giving our action a meaning beyond what we ourselves might give to it.

There are, however, limitations to this way of speaking. There is the danger that in picturing God as the Ultimate Agent we may come to denigrate human agency. Talk of an ultimate intention overriding our lesser intentions can easily slip into fatalism and the surrender of all initiative and responsibility. That would be an ironic conclusion considering that we took as our starting point the very agency which this conclusion seems to deny; yet that is a predicament into which this line of reasoning, if left unchecked, can easily fall. There is also the tendency with this model to lose sight of one's relationship to agents other than God. It is as though God's agency were solely directed to our good, as though his agency existed simply to undergird our own, when the biblical view is that God's intention is for the whole of creation.

Thus, even in developing the teleological motif, we must draw upon more than one model. The model of the elusive "I" is probably least in evidence, since the dominant concern of this motif is with the outcome of God's action and not with his or our subjectivity. Yet to ignore the subjective aspect altogether would be to reduce God to a process and ourselves to mere moments in the process. That would be contrary to the Christian understanding of God and man. The communal model comes into the picture when we consider that God's intention is not directed solely to our good, but to the good of the whole created order—the image of the Kingdom being the principal means by which this is expressed.

Still, in the main and subject to these qualifications, it is the intention-action model which gives the teleological motif its basic shape and form. The two qualifying models play a much larger role in the elaboration of the other two motifs: the dialogical and the ecological. The model of elusive subjectivity, for instance, is very important in a dialogical conception of God and man. For dialogue is something that takes place between subjects. Action alone cannot produce dialogue. The conception of God which emerges most clearly from this way of speaking is that of the Significant Other, the One whose presence gives significance and value to what we do. Of course, the dialogical motif is also necessary in order to identify God's action, since without some identifying word we would have no way of knowing what his intention toward us is. So we cannot think of the dialogical motif as having exclusively to do with subjectivity. We must continue to think of God as Agent.

The same is true of the ecological motif, in which the agency of God recedes even further into the background. It could easily lead to a conception of God simply as Subject out of all relationship to action of any kind or as the idealized Center of a system of relationship without any basis beyond itself. Yet that is not what we have in mind. Our intention in speaking this way is rather to place the agency of God in the context of other agencies—both personal and nonpersonal. It is a way of saying that our relationship with God is not simply on an I-Thou basis; it is set within a larger context of relationships in which he is the unifying factor. In the words of Niebuhr, he is the One beyond the many who gives unity to the many. He is still an Agent, but an Agent of a different order from other agents.

The decision to incorporate several different models into our thinking about God and his relationship to us may be highly significant in view of the pluralism of the present religious situation. For if it is the case that we are confronted with a range of different options, no one of which has an absolute claim on us, the best response may be to embrace this diversity and incorporate as many perspectives as possible into our thinking. It is important that there be one dominant model to give coherence and focus to our thinking, but to suppose there can be only one model would be to indulge in a kind of theological imperialism. In a situation of religious pluralism we need to be open to a variety of viewpoints without abandoning our own tradition. The use of different models in the interpretation of a single tradition may be the solution to that dilemma.

The technique of balancing off against one another different ways of speaking may also provide a clue to the traditional doctrine of the Trinity. Christians have always maintained that it is not three gods that they worship but one God apprehended in three distinct ways—as Father, Son, and Holy Spirit. If we think of God the Father as God in his ultimate transcendence, the One to whom all creatures are related simply in virtue of being creatures and who by virtue of his transcendence relates every creature to every other, we have something like the ecological motif. God the Son, on the other hand, is God in the mode of personal address and interaction, God in the person of Christ, coming among us and actively intervening on our behalf. This would correspond to what we have called the dialogical motif. God the Holy Spirit is God within us, guiding our actions, incorporating us into fellowship with others, giving us a basis for hope. This belongs to the teleological way of speaking.

Thus, rather than think of the doctrine of the Trinity as a highly speculative overbelief on the part of early Christians, we might rather think of it as a grammatical form, a "rule" for speaking Christianly of God. It makes explicit what would otherwise be implicit, that God even though he is One cannot be spoken of in only one way. In virtue of his ultimacy he eludes every sort of reductionism. If we try to speak of him in only one way, we invariably call forth a reaction of some sort; while if we deploy three different ways, we have a built-in corrective. We are less likely to fall into aberrations of one kind or another.

Ultimately, of course, God remains a mystery, but a mystery about which we can speak responsibly and meaningfully. We are not reduced to silence.

CONCLUSION

We are told that Jesus spoke with authority, though we also know that he was frequently misunderstood. In our own time the follower of Jesus would speak with authority if he could, but he is faced with a more pressing problem of communication. The conditions of our common life are such that it is difficult even to speak with another about one's faith. Religious pluralism together with secularization have tended to make faith in a transcendent reality an increasingly private, subjective sort of thing. Hence we are confronted by a dilemma: either we give up all reference to the transcendent or we cease being understood by others. The conditions for a common perception of "ultimate reality" are simply not there—or so it would seem.

The intent of this discussion has been to show that meaningful discourse about the transcendent is possible. It will not be in every respect like other forms of discourse: it can be expected to have its own logic. But neither can it be totally disparate, unrelated to other ways of thinking and speaking. For if we are to communicate at all with others, we must make contact with the larger universe of discourse in which they and we participate. What I have called the model of transcendence is a way of bridging this communications gap. Concepts borrowed from one sphere of discourse are adapted for use in another. More specifically, the terms in which we identify ourselves are extended to include identification of God.

In choosing from among various possible models of transcendence, we discover that communicability once again enters the picture. For there are ways of speaking of God which add to rather than detract from the problem. The model of the elusive "I," for instance, has enjoyed wide currency in the modern period largely because it enables us to speak of God in a way that is personal without being excessively mythological; yet it has also contributed to the subjectivization of religion by disposing us to view the transcendent as something inherently private. The only access we are supposed to have to

God is through our own subjectivity, which rules out any sort of corroborative judgment on the part of others and makes even minimal communication with others difficult. But supposing instead we take as our model the person as agent: that changes the picture considerably. Instead of being thrown back upon ourselves, we are directed to a world of activity outside of ourselves, a world which we share with others. Any talk of "God's action in the world" is going to involve interpretation, of course, but at least the basis for the interpretation is public rather than private. There is a way of indicating to others what it is we are talking about.

In addition to a particular model, we have committed ourselves to a particular religious tradition. That, too, raises problems of communication. For not everyone shares our religious tradition. In a pluralistic society, we cannot assume that everyone understands or accepts the biblical concepts and images. And even those who do may at times experience this tradition as something remote and alien. They may have difficulty assimilating it to their other ways of thinking and speaking or they may not see how it correlates with actual patterns of religious life; either way it will not be so meaningful as it ought to be if it is to function religiously. That is why systematic analysis of the tradition is important. By laying bare the conceptual principles of a tradition, the theologian makes it more accessible to others—both those outside the tradition and those within.

The tradition itself need not be thought of as fixed and rigid. It ought to possess that character of "open texture," which enables even concepts of a highly empirical sort to take on new meaning under changing conditions and circumstances. Neither ought we to suppose that the tradition must be monolithic, that it cannot accommodate a variety of perspectives. That is one reason for deploying more than one model: so we will not be trapped into a one-sided reading of the tradition. The important thing, though, is that we have a point of view which will get us inside our tradition, a way of regarding it which is not entirely alien to it. That is what we have tried to do with the model of personal agency. We have attempted to lay bare what might be called the conceptual foundations of the biblical-Christian tradition with a view to determining what can meaningfully be said about God within that tradition.

What emerges is a concept of God identifiable for both his freedom and his love. Why freedom? Because freedom is the perfection of agency. To be free is to be an agent in the fullest sense. It is to act with intention in all that one does, and therefore to be fully identified with one's action. Of God as of no other agent it can be said that he *is* what he *does*. Moreover, there is no limit to the scope of his action. It undergirds and interpenetrates everything that happens. Whereas we are inside our own action and outside the action of others, he is inside every action and outside of none. He is the Ultimate Agent, though not for that reason the only agent. On the contrary his freedom is at the basis of every other agent's freedom. In intending for the other he invests him with a capacity for action in his own right.

But then we must speak not only of freedom but of love. In intending for the other a good not his own, God shows his love for the other. His action may originate with himself, but it is directed toward the world. It has as its objective the creation of a world with its own intrinsic value. The extraordinary richness and fecundity of this creative love far exceeds our imagination, just as the freedom from which it proceeds eludes our conceptualization. Even its particularization in Christ does not exhaust the possibilities, though it does give a certain shape and direction to our expectations. Christ's action, we have said, is paradigmatic of God's action generally. It gives focus to what God is doing at all times everywhere.

But to conclude: Is this a meaningful way to speak of God or not? I should think that it is—both conceptually and personally. It is certainly not incongruent with our other ways of speaking, and in some respects it is quite integrative. For it draws together various conceptions we have of ourselves and our world and fits them into a unified framework of meaning. Not only that but it provides a transcendent grounding for some of our most basic values and ideals. Freedom and love, individuality and society, nature and history are all given a transcendent basis, according to this view.

To be sure, it is a viewpoint associated with a particular form of life; but that form of life is not in any sense narrow or parochial. It is unmistakably human. So in speaking of God we do not, after all, cut ourselves off from the larger human community. If there is a problem of communication, as there surely is, it is not because God is so transcendent, but because we are so fragmented and out of touch with our roots. What is needed is a deeper understanding of ourselves and of our world and a language appropriate to the mystery which encompasses both.

INDEX OF NAMES